"Desirée Gallimore's well-structu[...]ing will go a long way to alleviatir[...]that plague families and carers wher[...]for people with a disability. She sk[...], debunks many of the myths associated with independent travel whilst stressing the fact that it is a life-changing/door-opening event for people of all ages. This is an important and highly recommended book for all concerned with maximising the independence of every person with a disability."

—*Eileen Lyons, Department of Education, Transition to Post School for Students with Disabilities, Northern Sydney, Australia*

"In this excellent volume Dr. Desirée Gallimore gives the reader the understanding and confidence to teach students safe and independent travel. The book engagingly balances great expertise with solid common sense applied to a vitally important topic. Congratulations to author and publisher for producing a winner!"

—*Dr. Michael Farrell, private consultant in special education and author of* Educating Special Students, Third Edition

"This book is a must-read for everyone who provides travel instruction! An expert instructor describes the specialized teaching strategies and sequence of instruction she has used for decades. The case studies show how the crucial elements of an effective training program yield success. I recommend this invaluable resource to all of my colleagues."

—*Bonnie Dodson-Burk, Certified Orientation & Mobility Specialist, Pittsburgh Public Schools*

THE ESSENTIAL GUIDE TO SAFE TRAVEL-TRAINING FOR CHILDREN WITH AUTISM AND INTELLECTUAL DISABILITIES

of related interest

Achieving Successful Transitions for Young People with Disabilities
A Practical Guide
Jill Hughes and Natalie Lackenby
ISBN 978 1 84905 568 0
eISBN 978 1 78450 005 4

When Young People with Intellectual Disabilities and Autism Hit Puberty
A Parents' Q&A Guide to Health, Sexuality and Relationships
Freddy Jackson Brown and Sarah Brown
Foreword by Professor Richard Hastings
ISBN 978 1 84905 648 9
eISBN 978 1 78450 216 4

Toilet Training and the Autism Spectrum (ASD)
A Guide for Professionals
Eve Fleming and Lorraine MacAlister
Foreword by Penny Dobson
ISBN 978 1 84905 603 8
eISBN 978 1 78450 070 2

Transition and Change in the Lives of People with Intellectual Disabilities
Edited by David May
ISBN 978 1 85302 863 2
eISBN 978 1 84642 268 3

THE ESSENTIAL GUIDE TO SAFE TRAVEL-TRAINING FOR CHILDREN WITH AUTISM AND INTELLECTUAL DISABILITIES

Dr. Desirée Gallimore

Foreword by Dr. Mike Steer AM

Preface by Lizzie d'Avigdor and Martha d'Avigdor

Jessica Kingsley *Publishers*
London and Philadelphia

First published in 2017
by Jessica Kingsley Publishers
73 Collier Street
London N1 9BE, UK
and
400 Market Street, Suite 400
Philadelphia, PA 19106, USA

www.jkp.com

Library of Congress Cataloging in Publication Data
A CIP catalog record for this book is available from the Library of Congress

British Library Cataloguing in Publication Data
A CIP catalogue record for this book is available from the British Library

ISBN 978 1 78592 257 2
eISBN 978 1 78450 542 4

Printed and bound in the United States

To my brothers, Paul and Randall,
for their love, guidance, and questionable humor

Contents

Part 3: Travel-Training—Important Considerations

Foreword

Travel-training is, without doubt, one of the most important life skills a person with an intellectual disability can achieve. To be able to travel independently and safely gives individuals their freedom, and the ability to take control of their lives. It brings the person those feelings we all yearn for: happiness, self-worth, and self-fulfillment. Once achieved, it affects everyone in that person's life, whether it be amazement that independent travel was able to be achieved or recognition of the greatly enlarged life the person will now enjoy. It can also be a cause for self-reflection on our own beliefs about the ability of people, and the impact our limiting beliefs might have on the life aspirations of others. The aging parent who travel-trained their child to independence feels pride and relief that they will one day shuffle off this mortal coil with fewer worries, knowing that their child will be able to fully enjoy and access their life opportunities and be safe while doing so.

I recently caught a train at Central Station in downtown Sydney during the busy morning rush. I was sitting in a compartment and was approached by a well-dressed young man who wanted to share my seat. I moved over and he sat down. He wished me good morning and I him. He then continued listening to music through his headphones. This young man had Down syndrome yet in this workaday environment it didn't define him. It was no big deal. Yet Down syndrome once was. This helped me reflect on society's changing perception of people with a disability and the change in public perception that independent travel has generated.

So why has Dr. Gallimore written this remarkable book—the first of its kind about travel-training? Apart from being an authority on the subject, she has spent over 30 years actually practicing it. She believed it was time to share the "how to" as widely as possible so that children and adults with an intellectual disability can get on with their lives. I share her urgency. In this remarkable book, Dr. Gallimore has provided a step-by-step approach to travel-training. What we teach today will affect tomorrow, allowing our children, clients, and friends with intellectual disabilities innovative ways to live lives of enjoyment and accessibility, and to have the same sort of quality of life that we all value. I greatly enjoyed reading this book and learned a great deal from doing so. I am confident that you will too.

Dr. Mike Steer AM
Conjoint Senior Lecturer (Vision Impairment)
University of Newcastle
Australia

Preface

Lizzie: "Where are you Martha?"

"I'm on the train from Adelaide to Orange [1130 km/702 miles]! We've stopped at Broken Hill. I'm going to have dinner soon and what's more, I'm going to have a glass of wine with it!" The voice of my 36-year-old niece, almost squeaking with excitement, told me how much she was enjoying the journey. She was on her own, with not a care in the world.

Go back a few years, and the epiphanal moment etched forever in my brain was walking with 16-year-old Martha, down a street near our home, on our inaugural travel-training mission. Martha was going to learn how to get around independently. I soon realized how ill-equipped I was to guide Martha in negotiating these unfamiliar streets safely.

Martha had come to live with us from her home in Country New South Wales in order to take advantage of the fabulous special education facilities at the local secondary college. In my naiveté, it had not occurred to me to think through the nuts and bolts of how Martha was actually going to get to and from school independently.

So, I thought, it will just take a little time. I'll teach her how to get the bus. And how to cross the roads (how many are there?) to get to that bus. And where to get off the bus…and then how to get to school, and then how to do it all in reverse. The enormity of the challenge came to me within five minutes of leaving the house.

Martha and I reached our first road to be crossed. It was a complicated junction. Suddenly I was terrified for her. What is the point of saying look to your left? Are you always going to remember to do that? Will you look to your left again after looking to the right and then looking at oncoming cars—do you see there is a blinker on that means they are coming toward you as you are crossing, so look to your left again…

I knew that my fear would soon be imparted to Martha, even though she is the most cup-half-full person I know. It wasn't that she wasn't up to the task, it was me.

Fortunately, a friend listened to my wail and she made a reference to a service providing travel-training. She explained that travel-training is instruction designed to teach sighted people who have a disability the way to travel safely and confidently on routes in the community. Very soon after what must have sounded like a desperate phone call from a madwoman, someone appeared on my doorstep and said, "I am here to show Martha how to get around."

That someone was Desirée Gallimore.

From that moment on, I felt the burden of fear and worry lift from my shoulders. I was amazed that this service was available, and I felt completely privileged that we should be able to access it. I learned along with Martha how it was done.

The second epiphanal moment came three years later, after Martha had left us to return to her home in the Blue Mountains having completed her schooling. I opened the door one day to see her beautiful happy face, beaming with the smile of someone who fully knew the significance of what she had just achieved. She had walked to the train station in Katoomba, caught the train to Central, hailed the bus to Circular Quay, hopped on the ferry to Manly and then walked up the hill to our house in Fairlight (122km/76 miles). A four-hour, complicated journey, door to door, on her own.

That about summed it up for both of us.

Martha: I remember; it wasn't too bad that first time with Lizzie! But it was better with Desirée and she helped me a lot. After we caught the bus together, she would follow me to school just to make sure I got there. Once I forgot to get off the bus and went a long way—all the way to Hornsby! I wasn't scared. I was surprised to see Desirée there when I finally got off the bus and she drove me back. I didn't do that  again. Now I can travel all over the place, on buses and on trains, and it doesn't bother me at all. And it's good with the Metro cards now—I don't have to manage the right money. Sometimes when I went to school I would forget to keep it for the bus and spend it at the shop along the way.

I like to be able to get around on my own. Why not? You have to be able to get around! Now I go to work, to the library, to the café, and even traveled twice all the way from Adelaide to Orange and back, on the train. That was a long way. I read all my books from the library. It doesn't bother me at all. I can go anywhere. I adore Desirée.

Lizzie and Martha d'Avigdor

About the Author

Dr. Desirée Gallimore holds Master degrees in Psychology; Deafness and Communication; and Business Administration. She also has a Ph.D. in Education (Sensory Disability). Desirée is a psychologist (disability), a leading mobility specialist, and a published academic. She has worked in the profession of disability for over 30 years. Desirée is a specialist in travel-training/travel instruction for people who have multiple disabilities, assisting them to lead independent and self-directed lives. She has consulted in schools and communities in both developed and developing countries educating teachers, other professionals, and families about the methods and techniques of independent travel.

Acknowledgments

I am deeply grateful to my mentors and dear friends, particularly Frances Tinsley, Bronwyn Harrison, Lizzie d'Avigdor, Martha d'Avigdor, and Julia Kerr, for their tireless support, encouragement, and invaluable feedback throughout the stages of writing and editing this book. Thank you to my wonderful parents Patricia and Les Gallimore, my Aunty Bet (Howell), Don Berriman, and my brothers and their families for always loving me and believing in me.

Introduction

Do you want a family member, client, student, or friend to travel to work, to the shops, or to sporting and recreation events safely and independently? If so, then this book was written for you.

Over the past 30 years I have observed hundreds of parents, teachers, and other professionals working in the area of disability teaching their students and loved ones how to travel safely in the environment—a term known as "travel-training." They have worked incredibly hard, and spent many hours problem solving. Unfortunately, their programs often failed, usually because they did not have the relevant skills or knowledge. Learning the skills to travel-train is vital so that students can travel safely with minimal risks to themselves and to others.

The statistics on road safety are alarming, so it's natural that parents and service providers are worried about their child or student's safety. For example, in the Australian state of New South Wales, 22 percent of all fatal crashes involve a vehicle hitting a pedestrian, and closer to the larger cities of Sydney, Newcastle, and Wollongong this increases to 37 percent (more than one in every three fatal accidents).

So, what skills does the disability professional or parent need to learn? This book will answer that question. It will provide "insider" tips, strategies, and training techniques gathered over decades from working closely beside clients with multiple disabilities, their families, and professionals, which will equip the reader to become a successful travel-trainer.

A remark commonly made by people attending my training workshops is that they had no idea of what was really involved in teaching travel-training and were surprised by the precise and measured way in which travel-training is taught. Pleasingly, though, they also expressed relief that, once they had learned how to travel-train, it was a relatively straightforward process.

There are a number of myths surrounding travel-training that I've noticed over the years. Almost always, when I receive an enquiry from a teacher or parent and initially talk with them, I need to dispel some or all of these five myths.

Myth #1: *Anyone can teach travel-training skills without being trained.*

This, unfortunately, is not the case. There are specialized techniques, approaches, and tips involved in travel-training that trainers need to learn for a student's long-term success. These techniques are absolute essentials for successful travel-training programs.

Myth #2: *Travel-training starts in high school.*

Travel-training can start at *any* age—the earlier the better, and I've worked with babies with multiple disabilities. With very young children trainers can teach and model essential "foundation skills" in preparation for safe travel, road crossing, public transport travel, and other complex scenarios in later years (just as for children without a disability).

Myth #3: *Travel-training a student only takes a few weeks.*

Achieving a travel-training goal can take many weeks or months and sometimes over a year, depending on how complex the goal is and the student's confidence and previous experience. But training students so they are safe and retain the skills can be done in simple easy-to-achieve steps.

Myth #4: *Even if a student has never traveled alone, they can start travel-training on public transport.*

If a student has never traveled alone (i.e. independently), then the first travel-training priority is to develop foundation skills such as the way to seek assistance and avoid dangerous situations. These and other skills will assist the student (and family) to develop confidence and equip them to cope with confronting situations that will inevitably arise when traveling in more complex situations in the future.

Myth #5: *You only have to observe a student traveling a few times before they can travel by themselves.*

Even if you believe a student has learned how to get to a particular destination on their own and have observed them make this journey several times, there is a specific and measured process to know when to withdraw or "fade out" from the program. This process will allow you time to observe whether they have actually acquired the skills you taught and if they can use them when genuinely needed. For example, does the student: Use the mobile phone in an emergency? Cope when the bus gets diverted? Cross roads safely every single time? Find the way home if they are initially lost? If you fade out slowly in a measured way then there will be plenty of opportunities to observe whether or not the student applies these skills 100 percent of the time.

My motivation to specialize in travel-training comes from the first person I ever trained. Deborah helped me realize what an essential life skill independent travel is. One day she presented me with a small piece of paper. On it, drawn in faded blue ink, was the stick figure image of two smiling girls—her and me—each on a swing. Deborah had drawn the picture 11 months after she'd left an institution where she'd lived since she was just two months old. Fourteen years later Deborah, who had only a mild intellectual disability, left the institution for the first time to live in a group home in the community. In her 14 years at the institution, she had never ventured beyond the front door.

That was in 1986 and the policy of "de-institutionalization" was being rolled out across Australia. I was 19 years old, a naïve first-year university student who'd volunteered in one of the first group homes for people with disabilities in a small rural town. Remarkably, I was given the job of meeting Deborah at the institution's gate, walking the few streets with her to her new home and making her familiar with "all" aspects of independent travel.

Deborah was tolerant and kind during the year we spent together. She smiled at my efforts to explain the mechanics of pedestrian crossings and the "walk/don't walk" flashing signals. She laughed when I got tongue-tied explaining the purpose of money and how to buy items in shops.

Walking home one afternoon from a travel-training session, she suggested we stop at a park for a swing and some fun. During the hour on the swings in the park that summer's afternoon, I realized some of the invaluable lessons Deborah had taught me. She showed me what happens to a person when they move from dependence to independence: they emerge motivated, happy, and hopeful, with the realized possibility of a bigger life. They observe the impact their independence has on others and see the positive shift in people's attitudes toward them, however subtle. They see people's respect for their ability, they feel people's trust and they realize they have freed others from obligation. They are free to develop and redefine themselves as individuals in the world.

Toward the end of our swing in the park that afternoon, Deborah stopped and briefly touched my hand. "I've learned many things...for the first time," she said quietly. The next day, before she walked down to meet a friend at the cinema, she handed me the drawing of us on the swings. "This is us," Deborah smiled, "I drew it for you. It's us having fun...and me feeling free."

There are three parts to the book, which I recommend you read in succession. First, "Travel-Training: The Essentials" explains why travel-training is the *most important skill* for a person with a disability to learn, and includes the five "must-know" key steps for a successful travel-training program. Second, "Travel-Training: The Ingredients" expands on the five "must-know" steps, showing you how to deliver successful travel-training programs to all your students, regardless of their travel experience. Third, "Travel-Training: Important Considerations" includes a range of tips and solutions to common travel-training problems that you will inevitably face. I have included case studies that will guide you through the steps to teach beginner, intermediate, and advanced travelers.

Throughout the book I use "student" to refer to the person being taught travel-training skills regardless of whether a professional or parent is providing the training. I've also used "trainer" to cover anyone who delivers training—usually a parent, teacher, or disability worker.

This book will provide you with the information you need to start travel-training. I also encourage you to pass your knowledge on to others to equip them to travel-train their students. As Anthony Greenbank wisely observed in *The Book of Survival*, "To live through an impossible situation, you don't need the reflexes of a Grand Prix driver, the muscles of Hercules, the mind of Einstein. You simply need to know what to do."[1]

---

1   Anthony Greenbank (2003) *The Book of Survival: The Original Guide to Staying Alive in the City, the Suburbs and the Wild Lands Beyond.* New York: Hatherleigh Press (first published 1968).

Part 1

TRAVEL-TRAINING
THE ESSENTIALS

"The best time to plant a tree was 20 years ago. The second best time is now."

Chinese proverb

1

A Life Priority: Safe and Independent Travel

Most of us were taught safe techniques to travel in public from a very young age, through explanation and/or observation. For example, when we walked to the shop for the first few times we depended on a family member or friend to take us. Initially, we might not have noticed the route we took to get there. But when we arrived at the shop for the first time we learned that it sold all sorts of delicious delights. Then we *really* wanted to keep going to the shop and it became a conscious goal to get there. In time, we began to learn the safest way to cross the road, which path to take, which direction to go in, and what to do in the shop to make a purchase. Finally, we walked to the shop by ourselves and become an independent traveler on this route. We could then generalize many of these skills to other routes, and through experience, became the independent travelers we are today.

However, there are many people in our community who are not taught this essential life skill. They are our sons, daughters, friends, and students with disabilities who have never learned how to travel independently. This opportunity has not been withheld deliberately but rather as a result of difficult circumstance and loving intention. For instance, specialist teachers working with many students with disabilities at one time are concerned about student safety, and are limited in the number and type of travel experiences they can provide their students. Further, most parents of a child with a disability very naturally protect their offspring by holding their hand across the road, telling them when it is safe to cross the road, driving them to the shops and other activities, buying items for them at the shop, and doing as much as possible for the child well into their teenage years and beyond, with the purpose of making their life easier. Unfortunately, the day eventually comes when the parent, often through older age or ill health, can no longer take their (adult) child to work, to the shops, or to recreational activities. The questions that arise at this point are "Who will take my son to work?" "Who will take him on outings?" "What's going to happen to my child?"

I have seen hundreds of these scenarios and usually there is no satisfactory answer to these questions in the short term. Often, no one else is available to take their family member to work, to the shops, or to recreational activities. The consequence for dependent family members is devastating. Their life shrinks and they live day by day within their home, with little or no access to the world or the activities they once enjoyed. Their quality of life dramatically decreases and the negative impact of this on the person's health and happiness is significant.

However, the good news is that regardless of the type of disability, all people can enjoy safe travel—and travel-training can start at *any* age. With training, children grow into able adults who can take themselves wherever they want to go. A wonderful byproduct of independent travel for individuals is the remarkable increase in self-confidence that affects all aspects of their lives in positive and far-reaching ways. Before travel-training many young people who learned to travel independently were quiet, lacked confidence, and were sometimes withdrawn. After travel-training these same people were motivated to learn other routes, would instigate discussions or activities, spoke easily with people who were unfamiliar to them, and were happier people all round. Almost always when this happens, parents are incredibly surprised at their child's ever-increasing confidence, motivation, and ability to interact and manage in the world.

There are five consecutive steps in a successful travel-training program. They include:

1. Understand your student.

2. Establish the travel-training goal.

3. Plan the route prior to teaching.

4. Teach the planned route.

5. Fade out and allow your student to travel independently.

These steps seem fairly straightforward and will be discussed at greater length throughout the book. However, the most common mistakes made by trainers are either diverting from these five steps, or not teaching all that's involved in each step. For example, the trainer might disregard the original goal and, during training, expand or complicate it beyond reason so that the student can never achieve the goal; or teaching might occur in segments that are too large or delivered too quickly (which prevents the student from learning); or trainers finish the program too early without going through the correct procedures of fading out from the program. The important message here is if you follow the five steps of travel-training and all that is involved in each step, then you will be able to teach your student to travel safely.

It is important to mention that the majority of students, even before travel-training, have incidentally acquired a few prerequisite travel-training skills. Students develop some understanding of "how the world works" through practical experience and observation of other people's behavior. Children are "sponges," and we are rarely completely aware of how much information they absorb about their world. For example, some older students know that moving vehicles are dangerous and will be cautious or reluctant to walk in front of one, and others know that waiting at road edges or at traffic lights holds some kind of importance (even if they don't know why). The majority of students have strong self-preservation and survival instincts that prevent them from deliberately putting themselves in harm's way. During travel-training we can discover, observe, and shape this knowledge and build upon it so that students can eventually travel safely and independently.

KEY POINTS

» A person can begin travel-training at *any* age. It is never too early or too late to learn.

» Successful travel-training is based on the five consecutive steps and teaching all that is involved in each step. The steps are:

1. Understand your student.

2. Establish the travel-training goal.

3. Plan the route prior to teaching.

4. Teach the planned route.

5. Fade out and allow your student to travel independently.

» Many students come to travel-training with some knowledge or experience. They have already observed other people's travel behavior and developed instincts of self-preservation.

» Travel-training is an essential life skill enabling people to live their lives now and in the future (when they might have fewer support systems around them).

2

How to Achieve Safe and Independent Travel

"Where do you want your son or daughter to travel when they're 18, 25, 40, or 50 years old?" This is usually the first question I ask parents attending a travel-training workshop or when meeting them for the first time in their home. Parents are typically surprised or confused when I ask them this question, and don't know how to respond.

Many parents of a child with a disability never contemplate how or where their child might travel on their own. Often parents are simply coping with the everyday administration of life. While they obviously think about life for their child 10, 20, or 30 years into the future, they are not sure how to go about making their son or daughter as independent as possible. As well, it would be fair to say that most parents err on the side of protecting their child rather than encouraging them—or even allowing them—to take even moderate levels of risk.

Yet considering this question is one of the pivotal moments when their child's future is determined. It is the point where parents decide whether their child will become a fully independent traveler, and be able to control aspects of their own working and leisure lives. If the parent, at this moment, perceives that it's too hard or too risky, then the child will in all likelihood remain dependent. If the parent perceives the possibility of independence with guidance, then the child will most likely go on to attain safe traveling skills.

Trust in your mind

Our mind and our thoughts determine our reality. If we stop a moment to think about people who are successful, they all share one characteristic. They *believe* in themselves and they *believe* they can. Some of the most absurd ideas have become reality. In 1903 it is generally accepted that the Wright brothers (rather than the aviator Gustave Whitehead) flew the first power-driven, pilot-controlled, heavier-than-air machine. Of course it did not happen overnight. They argued, theorized, philosophized, and probably did not talk to each other for weeks. However, if we look up to the sky now we'll see or hear the result of their self-belief. Orville Wright reflected, "If we worked on the assumption that what is accepted as true really is true, then there would be little hope for advance."

There are thousands of examples of success arising from people's self-belief. For example, Harland Sanders, reflecting on founding Kentucky Fried Chicken (KFC), said:

> I made a resolve then that I was going to amount to something. And no hours, nor amount of labor, or amount of money would deter me from giving my best that there was in me. And I have done that ever since, and I win by it. I know.

"Colonel" Sanders was in his early sixties when he founded KFC. He had dropped out of school at seventh grade, was a soldier in the US Army, and at age 40 was a cook in a service station. Mahatma Gandhi simply stated, "You must be the change you want to see in the world," and Henry Ford, founder of the Ford Motor Company, said, "Whether you think you can or think you can't—you are right."

The power of words

The words we use to express our beliefs largely determine whether or not we will be successful. There are powerful words and there are weak words. Powerful words like "That's possible," "I can," "I will," "I'll do it," "It'll work" are often followed by success. Weak words such as "I can't," "I won't," "It's hard," "I'll never," "That's impossible" are usually followed by failure. In order to be successful, we must be mindful of the words we use, and use only positive powerful words.

Parents of people with disability sometimes use weak words, especially if they are worried about their child's safety. One mother wanted her 21-year-old son to walk a short route from home to the shop at the corner of their street. Her son had a mild learning impairment, was attentive, and very keen to learn the route. I worked with the mother for several months on the travel route, explaining and demonstrating the techniques required for her to teach her son to walk to and from the shop safely and independently. Despite her son being able to easily achieve walking this route independently, after a few weeks the mother's language signaled the eventual outcome of this travel-training program. She commented, "I don't think I've got time to teach him"; "It's too hard to do the training once a week"; "I can't train him anymore." Despite me offering simple solutions to the challenges she raised, the mother continued to believe she could not teach her son. Maybe she was worried about his safety, maybe she felt she didn't have the skills she needed to teach him, and maybe her life was very busy. Needless to say, the son did not learn to travel the route. Ten years on he continued to be driven to destinations and dependent on his parents. If she had invested in the original program that included important travel-training foundation skills, then it is likely that her son would now be traveling by himself to work and recreational activities.

In contrast, a father wanted his 23-year-old son to travel independently to work. The route was a complex one. The son would need to walk from home to a busy bus stop, catch a bus that terminated far from his workplace, and walk the long route to work. During the walk to work, the son needed to cross two busy roads. The son had a significant intellectual disability and was extremely strong willed, believing he did not need travel-training. He had never traveled on a bus, or crossed roads independently. This was a highly complex situation, and the father faced many challenges. However, from the outset his language was powerfully positive and full of determination. "I'll work with him weekly," He'll learn it," "When he crosses here at this point, it's easy," "We'll use your approach and it'll work." This travel route took some time to teach. However, within a year, the son was traveling to work safely, reliably, and independently.

Your future is created today

The main emotions that limit us are fear and self-doubt. If we do not consciously repel these emotions then they will be reflected in our thoughts, our words, and our actions. If we allow these emotions to rule us, then achieving travel-training goals will be very difficult. As trainers, we need to become self-aware and observe the emotions we feel and the actions we take. If we want to teach a travel route to a student, but are overcome by fear before starting, then we need to ask ourselves "Why?" "Why am I feeling scared?" "Why am I allowing this feeling of fear to overwhelm me?" "What am I fearful of?"

Often fear is the result of unfamiliarity. We feel fear because we do not know how to react or deal with a situation. If we fear teaching a person how to cross a road, then it is because we either haven't learned how to teach the skill, or don't trust our own ability to teach the skill correctly. However, this fear fades when we have learned the right strategies to teach a skill *and* we believe we can teach the skill.

If we doubt that we are capable of teaching a travel route, then we cannot teach it. If we believe we can, then we will. Remarkably, it is as simple as that. As a trainer, if you are confronted with your mind's talk of self-doubt, stop these thoughts immediately and be aware that you are allowing yourself to doubt yourself.

Immediately replace these thoughts of self-doubt with thoughts of self-belief—quickly and decisively. If you catch yourself thinking, "I can't teach him how to cross this road—he's too dependent on me," consciously replace this with "I can teach him to cross this road. I just need to follow the simple strategy that I have learned to teach this skill." Immediately replace self-doubt talk with positive "I-can-do" thoughts.

The most difficult aspect of teaching a travel route is committing your time and yourself to teaching. Teaching someone to travel independently is like following a recipe—it is not difficult. However, unless you are prepared to invest by committing to making a time each week to teach, then your student will not achieve independent travel. If you say, "I don't have time this week," or "I was too tired," then your travel-training goals will never be realized. Your future is created today.

It's your decision

Ask yourself, "Am I ready to learn skills and strategies to teach independent travel?" This question needs some serious contemplation. If your answer is "Yes, I'm ready," then you have made a serious commitment.

However, if your answer is "No—I'm not ready to learn the skills and strategies to teach independent travel" then this book is not for you right now. It might be that you prefer another person to teach your client, child, or family member. Regardless of the trainer, that person will need to commit 100 percent of themselves before successful, safe, and independent travel can take place.

The five consecutive steps of travel-training

1. **Understand your student:** Each student has strengths and traits, skills and motivations, which will influence the program's goal, the travel route, and the way you teach the route. Knowing your student and understanding who

the student is as a person is possibly the most important step in delivering a successful travel-training program. *There is no such thing as a generic travel-training program.*

2. **Establish the travel-training goal:** A travel-training goal is an intention with a specific beginning and end. For example: Pat will walk the route from home to her corner shop to purchase an item of choice.

3. **Plan the route prior to teaching:** This step involves investigating the safest route, then considering the best way to teach it to a specific student, for example, investigating the safest walking route from home to a specific shop, then deciding to teach that route in small, defined segments.

4. **Teach the planned route:** Teach the student the specific planned route using training techniques tailored to that student.

5. **Fade out and allow your student to travel independently:** After teaching the planned route, the trainer "fades out" or slowly withdraws from training using the correct procedure (i.e. setting a performance criterion), after which the student is able to travel the route safely.

Each of the five steps needs to be completed for an individual to achieve safe and independent travel on a particular route.

Applying the five steps of travel-training

When I was teaching Pam to assist her 18-year-old son Mike to walk to the mall independently, we used these five steps to keep us focused on the task. When Pam initially contacted me, Mike depended on her to walk with him to the mall. Mike had a learning impairment and autism, and felt uncomfortable being alone in public.

After discussions with Pam and Mike about their travel-training wants and needs:

- I assessed Mike's current abilities, traits, and interests (step 1).

- We defined a goal (step 2). Mike's goal was to walk to the mall independently, purchase his favorite car magazine at the newspaper shop, and walk back home. Pam believed she could teach Mike this route. She was committed to learning travel-training strategies and giving time once a week to Mike's training.

- Pam and I met at her home and together walked the route to investigate and plan the safest route to the newspaper shop (step 3). (Planning is central to achieving goals. If we think of a goal that we have not achieved, then it is often because the goal was not followed by a well-thought-out and executed plan.) After walking the route together, we divided it into eight small segments and agreed which segment she would teach Mike first. During the planning session, I taught Pam a range of training strategies and provided her with many travel-training tips.

- Once the goal for travel-training had been determined, and a thorough and well-considered plan of action had been defined, Pam commenced teaching the route (step 4). She methodically progressed through each step of the plan. Pam applied the relevant teaching strategies and approaches described in Chapters 5, 6, and 8. She believed in her ability to teach, used positive powerful words, and was consistent in her training approach.

- Once Pam had taught each step of the travel-training plan, she faded out from teaching. Mike then had the skills and confidence to travel the route safely and independently (step 5).

If you want your family member, student, or client to be traveling in future years and: are committed to learning strategies and techniques of independent travel; are prepared to use powerful and positive words; believe in your ability to teach; are committed to giving a small amount of time each week to training, then you are ready to apply the information in this book.

KEY POINTS

» The most powerful determinant of whether a travel-training program will be successful is the mental approach of the person delivering the training. The thoughts that arise from our mind determine our reality. If we use positive thoughts such as "I can train my son to cross this road" or "I will apply the travel-training techniques I have learned" then you will be able to teach these skills. However, if you have negative thoughts and use negative language such as "I don't have time to teach this skill" or "I can't teach my son how to travel on a bus" then you will not teach travel-training skills successfully.

» If you experience fear and doubt when delivering a travel-training program then this is usually because you are unfamiliar with the way to teach a skill. Once you have learned how to teach travel-training skills, and believe you can, the fear and doubt will fade.

» Think of where your student might want to travel in ten years' time (work and leisure activities). The travel skills you teach today are the building blocks, enabling your student to achieve their future travel goals.

» Follow the five steps of travel-training and apply the techniques described and you will deliver successful travel-training programs.

Part 2

TRAVEL-TRAINING
THE INGREDIENTS

"Leap and the net will appear."

Zen saying

3

Establishing the Travel-Training Goal

In 1993, I took a stroll on a freezing December morning in Simla, in the Himalayan mountains in India. Soon after I left for my walk it was bucketing snow. Suddenly, there were no distinguishing environmental features to help me orient myself— just white uniform mountains all around. I had no idea which direction I had come from, or which way was home. After about 20 minutes I started to panic. I turned and saw a small dot appear on the horizon. Within minutes, before me was a very old man dressed in the brightest of saffron robes. He was warm and kind and simply pointed in the direction of home. He chuckled and whispered, leaning his spectacled face toward mine, "We cannot begin until we know where we are going." And so it is with goals. We need a goal if we are to achieve a goal. An important step in travel-training is identifying a precise and clear goal.

What's a goal?

Of course, we all know what a goal is. It seems patronizing to even define it. But goals can be slippery. They can get away from us, even though we think we have defined them and shaped them into a manageable size.

A goal is an intention with a specific beginning and end. A travel-training goal needs to be (i) relevant, (ii) rewarding, (iii) achievable, (iv) realistic, taking into account the student's strengths and weaknesses. So what does this actually mean? Consider the following example:

Zac is 18 years old, and has Asperger syndrome and an intellectual disability. He particularly dislikes loud noise, talking with people, activities that involve crowds and people sitting close to him. He is frightened of dogs and thunder. Zac likes to concentrate on one activity at a time. He enjoys playing computer games, swimming in his pool, and reading about model trains. Zac enjoys his own company and the company of his immediate family, though preferably on a one-to-one basis. He has never traveled independently. His mum has set a goal for Zac to travel independently from his home to the city's major cinema complex—the goal involves traveling on a bus and a ferry. Unfortunately, Zac will probably never accomplish this goal. Why? Because the following questions have not been considered.

Does the route have relevance to Zac? Answer: No.

It is highly unlikely that Zac would want to visit a cinema complex that is loud, crowded, and disorderly. He will not be motivated to learn this route; it will lack relevance for him.

Would learning the route be rewarding for Zac? Answer: No.

A cinema complex would be the least likely place Zac would prefer to be. He would possibly instigate a range of negative behaviors to avoid traveling to this destination.

Is this goal achievable? Answer: No.

Zac has never traveled anywhere independently (i.e. alone). He is unfamiliar with being on his own in public. Being alone in public would be emotionally demanding and confronting for him. To feel comfortable and confident in public, he would need to learn a range of coping mechanisms (e.g. strategies to cope with crowds, aggressive or curious dogs, and thunder on stormy days) and risk-management strategies (e.g. what to do if the bus/train broke down, phone strategies to seek assistance, how to create space around himself when he needed this). Zac would also be too overwhelmed with the size of the route and the amount of learning involved in traveling on multiple forms of transport within one journey. Equally, the amount of learning required and the number of people Zac would need to interact with along this lengthy route would be aversive to him.

Is this goal realistic? Answer: No.

The goal is too large for Zac, and involves too much training and time to hold the long-term attention of Zac or his trainer. The training goal does not take into account Zac's strengths and weaknesses, or his likes and dislikes.

Considerations to help establish a relevant and achievable travel-training goal

Before a travel-training goal can be identified, the trainer needs to consider what travel skills the student currently has. Obviously, if the student already independently crosses roads and travels on buses, then a travel goal to a new location can include these travel skills.

However, if the student has never traveled anywhere alone, then a small walking route to a destination close to home, or a similar uncomplicated route, is a reasonable starting point. The following questions need to be considered to help establish a relevant and realistic travel-training goal. Student examples are provided to help illustrate the points being made.

Has the student ever traveled independently?

This question helps to determine how big or small to make the travel-training goal. For example, if Sue has never traveled independently, then regardless of her abilities, it will be a priority for her to first learn to feel comfortable and confident "alone in the environment."

Imagine Sue has an intellectual disability and is able to walk confidently, ahead of the trainer, to the corner shop. That is a good achievement. However, Sue knows that the trainer is behind her and feels confident that he will "save" her should any untoward event occur such as being approached by a dog. It's likely that the trainer has already "saved" her in some way on previous occasions. Perhaps Sue once took an incorrect turn on the route and he stopped her and showed her the correct way to go. Perhaps, when walking ahead, Sue sometimes looks back at him for reassurance. If Sue was walking to the shop and he suddenly disappeared, then most likely she would panic, lose her confidence, and be reluctant to walk this route again. Therefore, if we were to set a travel goal for Sue, it would be a small goal. For instance, Sue's goal might be to walk from the school gate to the corner shop, and then return to school. There are no road crossings on this route and it takes only a few minutes to walk. This small travel goal would allow Sue to build confidence in her abilities quickly as she is learning to travel independently in her familiar local environment. Also, the route would only take a short time to teach, so Sue would experience a sense of accomplishment in a relatively short period of time. Most importantly, Sue would have learned to be in the environment by herself, a prerequisite for independent travel and more complicated mobility goals.

Conversely, if Darren already travels independently to school, the mall, and the beach using buses, then with time and experience he has developed self-confidence and travel skills. Therefore, the next goal for Darren could be larger. If Darren wanted to travel from his home to a friend's place, a journey that included two buses and numerous road crosses, then he would most likely succeed as he has self-confidence and has learned bus travel skills, emergency strategies, and road crossing skills in earlier travel-training programs.

Where does the student need to travel?

Years ago I was contacted by a special education teacher. He was training a student with a physical and intellectual disability to walk from her classroom to the office within the school. It was a lengthy route and required the student to use considerable concentration and physical effort. The teacher remarked that the student was not progressing in learning the route, and he had to "insist" she learn to travel this route. When I visited the teacher at the school to discuss the situation I asked, "Why does she need to walk from her classroom to the office?" The teacher hesitated for a moment, then explained that it was simply a "good excuse" to practice her travel skills.

Like all of us, people with disabilities recognize when their time and energy is being wasted or when a task is irrelevant to them. Our time and effort is precious, and none of us like that to be taken for granted. And so it was for this student. She recognized that there was no good reason for her to walk this difficult route from her classroom to the office, and that it was a waste of her energy and time. She was not progressing as she was resisting doing a pointless task. When I watched her walking the route, she appeared to be deliberately making wrong turns to torment her teacher! I admired her intelligent and effective strategy of retaliation.

Before choosing any travel goal we must consider what type of travel routes the student might want or need to travel when they are, for example, 20, 30, or 50 years of age. If a person will never travel anywhere unaccompanied (say, because of a particular need for physical support) then there is no point in attempting to teach that person to travel independently. It is a waste of their time and yours. Instead, perhaps this person lacks the confidence to walk down stairs, so it would be an excellent goal to teach them to use stairs, helping to increase their self-confidence. Or perhaps a person with a physical disability needs to learn how to walk confidently across uneven ground surfaces (concrete to grass; grass to rocky ground), or travel with confidence in crowds. Another option is to teach them to make decisions about traveling by using timetables. All of these scenarios make excellent training goals because they are skills that benefit the student now and into the future. We only need to teach travel skills that satisfy a person's travel needs. Your student will definitely appreciate and respond to a useful and purposeful travel goal.

Some months ago, the mother of a 15-year-old girl, Claire, contacted me. Claire had Down syndrome and was an effervescent, happy person. Her mother realized that in a few years she would leave school and perhaps work as an assistant in a kindergarten or in the food service industry. Claire's family lived in a small suburb away from larger centers that might contain job opportunities for her. Her mother realized that she would most probably need to take a bus to these larger suburbs to get to work. Claire had never traveled anywhere independently.

As the future travel expectation for Claire was that she would take local buses to work, travel-training had to respond to this need. However, as she had never traveled anywhere alone, the first training goal was a short one close to home with the intent of building Claire's self-confidence when traveling.

The first travel-training goal we set for Claire was to walk from home to the local bakery to buy her favorite pastry. The bakery was only two streets away from home. This route was reduced into small teaching segments. Claire learned to travel this small route independently, which helped to increase her self-confidence. Confidence is a prerequisite to learning more complex skills such as bus travel and traveling independently to other destinations.

Alternatively, if there was no destination close to Claire's home where she wanted to travel independently, we would need to be a little more creative. Remember, the first travel route is for the purpose of building Claire's self-confidence when traveling alone in public. In this situation, we would identify what interests Claire had, for example, bowling on a Saturday morning. In this scenario, the travel goal might be for Claire to walk independently from the entrance gate of the bowling club (her mother would drive her to the club, park the car, and walk with Claire to the gate) to the counter where she pays for her bowling session, receives her bowling shoes, and puts them on. Her mother would then meet her for her game of bowls.

Although this might not be perceived as a long mobility route, it has its complexities. For the first time in her life, Claire would learn to walk independently into a business, request a service from a stranger, negotiate payment, and receive items which she would manipulate in preparation for her activity. Once Claire has learned skills such as these, her self-confidence will increase markedly. She might then learn similar routes such as walking from the mall entrance to her favorite shop to buy an item, or from the car park into a corner shop to purchase an item. Confidence is the necessary foundation upon which more complex travel-related skills and routes can be taught.

Is the student motivated to travel?

Occasionally, frustrated teachers ask me, "What can I do to make my student travel a route?" A typical scenario: "When we go travel-training to the local shops, my student [name] does not want to go. When he knows it's time to go, he sits on the floor in the classroom refusing to move. Or if we do manage to get him out the door, he sits down in the street or sometimes he runs away."

Trainers need to recognize and acknowledge the wants and needs of their students. If a student does not want to travel on a route, then the student will find any way to escape traveling.

If a student lacks the motivation to travel on a route, then we need to ask why. There's always a reason why a student is not motivated to travel. It is our job to discover that reason. Once we identify the reason, we can start to work on solutions to encourage the student's engagement in travel-training. Some common reasons why students have not wanted to engage in travel-training include: they receive far more attention from teachers when they refuse to go; they are scared to cross roads; they dislike the teacher who will accompany them; they dislike the student(s) who accompanies them; they are enjoying another activity that they do not want to stop; they do not enjoy purchasing items at a shop; they feel pressured to perform tasks that they do not have the skills to perform; they feel embarrassed walking with other students with disabilities; they believe their travel skills exceed those in which they are asked to engage; the route is too lengthy; or they feel unwell.

Is the student emotionally ready for travel-training?

We must consider whether or not the student is emotionally ready to engage in travel-training. As teachers and parents of people with disabilities, you will already be aware that their chronological age does not necessarily equal their emotional age.

An employment agency once asked me to travel-train 19-year-old Ben who had a significant intellectual impairment. Ben had recently finished school and was excited about starting work. After Ben had been working for three weeks the agency wanted him to learn to walk the short route from his home to his workplace. Upon observing Ben over a number of walks to work, it was evident that he was behaving impulsively and was unable to concentrate when crossing a narrow road. Instead, he would rush out onto the road regardless of whether a car was present, and would run instead of walk during the route.

It was clear that Ben was a capable person. At work he enjoyed gardening and was able to patiently and methodically prepare the earth before planting seeds with minimal assistance. He also had organizational skills and kept the potting shed orderly and clean. Ben also enjoyed cooking. He was able to follow simple recipes using photographs that illustrated the step-by-step preparation process.

I realized that Ben was overexcited about walking to work. His excitement overtook his usual methodical and patient approach to acquiring skills. At work, he was being exposed to many new people and jobs, and had become saturated with new experiences.

Ben was not emotionally ready at that point for a new learning opportunity such as travel-training. Instead, I revisited Ben six months later. By that time, he had settled into the routine of work and was familiar with his role and colleagues. This time when we walked the route, Ben was calmer and receptive to learning. He was able to concentrate and walked the route instead of running. He had matured emotionally, partly as a result of his work experiences and a broadening of his social activities. Ben learned to walk this route safely and independently within three months of training.

We can only "go with the flow" of our students. It does not matter if a person is 8 years old, 25 years old, or older when they commence travel-training. If students are not emotionally ready to learn travel-training skills, then pushing or forcing them will only make travel-training a negative experience and one they might try to avoid in the future. Our intention is for students to enjoy travel-training and not even necessarily know they are being trained. Travel-training needs to be an easy and pleasurable experience. Travel-training is about harnessing the person's motivation and ability and channeling that toward developing skills. It is an opportunity for students to experience their ability, intelligence, capability, and freedom. However, we need to listen to and observe the students. They will tell us through their words and actions when they are ready to commence travel-training.

Can the student cross roads independently?

Local authorities often provide guidelines about the appropriate age for children to cross roads independently. In NSW, Australia, the government cites that children have the capacity and maturity to judge traffic and cross roads independently at about 12 years of age. Often people with a learning impairment or other disabilities might be older than the suggested 12 years before their judgment has matured enough for them to make successful road crossing decisions.

Regardless, road crossing training can commence very early in a child's life. For example, a travel-training program can be developed for a two-year-old that includes observing a family member deliberately role-model the way to cross on a variety of different road types. It's never too early to learn.

There are many different types of road crossings. The major crossing types include:

- **Controlled crossings:** These are automated, such as the audio-tactile signals (ATS) or traffic light signals. The ATS have an audible "beep" that quickens when it is safe to cross. Once you have pressed the button on the ATS, leave your hand on it. You will notice a tactile "thud" in your hand that quickens when it is safe to cross. These ATS were designed for people who are deaf (hence the tactile signal in the hand) or vision impaired (hence the audible signal).

- **Pedestrian crossings:** A specific place designated for pedestrians to cross the road, often, though not always, evident by broad white stripes on the road.

- **Uncontrolled crossings:** These roads are neither controlled by ATS traffic signals nor by pedestrian crossings. These uncontrolled roads need to be negotiated by simply identifying when it is safe to cross. There are no legal requirements at this time in Australia, the UK, and the US for vehicles to stop for pedestrians at uncontrolled crossings.

While it is a relatively straightforward process to teach a person to cross a road, trainers need to consider the correct time to introduce road crossing training. Road crossing requires a degree of self-confidence. If a person has never traveled a route independently, then it's likely that they will feel confronted and experience self-doubt during road crossing training. Remember, travel-training needs to be fairly stress free. Training needs to be enjoyable for the student and trainer. Therefore, before introducing road crossing, consider teaching the person to walk a short route independently that does not include road crosses. As discussed previously, it might be a small route within a shopping center or a walking route to the park or shop near the person's home. Introduce short travel routes that the person learns to travel independently, before introducing increasingly complex skills such as road crossing.

What medical aspects might affect travel-training?

I arrived at a high school one morning to meet my student with Down syndrome for a travel-training lesson. The 13-year-old student had progressed in road crossing training and had started making reliable and independent road crossing decisions on uncontrolled roads. When the student met me at the office that morning, she appeared vague and unusually quiet, and was moving slowly. This was unusual behavior for this typically energetic and communicative girl.

Talking with her teacher, I learned that her medication had recently changed and the new medication was affecting her behavior. Therefore, I chose not to train the student that day, delaying training for three weeks until her medication had stabilized and she had returned to her usual personality. The risks of training a student when affected by medication are significant. The student might make incorrect travel decisions, which might compromise her safety. Avoid training students when they are affected by medication or appear unwell.

There are a range of medical conditions that will typically affect the travel-training goal or the method of training a student. Although not an exhaustive list, such conditions include a person with an intellectual disability also having: an acquired brain injury (ABI); a learning disability; an anxiety disorder; or attention deficit hyperactivity disorder (ADHD). If a person has vision impairment, then consult orientation and mobility (O&M) agencies specializing in this profession.

Generally, these conditions do not prevent a student from learning to travel independently. However, they might influence the training goal that is chosen, how the route is divided into easy-to-learn segments, or the type of assistance the trainer provides.

Acquired brain injury

Acquired brain injury describes damage to the brain after birth. There are three major types of ABI: first, ABI acquired as a result of a cerebro-vascular accident (CVA) (that is, a stroke) where a blood vessel has blocked or ruptured causing damage to the brain because of the interruption to blood flow; second, drug- or alcohol-related ABI where substance abuse has led to brain damage; third, traumatic brain injury (TBI) that results from a blow to the head (e.g. in a vehicle accident) or a penetrating head injury (e.g. a gunshot wound). Brain injury can also occur as a result of tumors, illness, or when breathing stops for a significant period of time.

People with an ABI often have cognitive impairments affecting specific areas of functioning. The effects of brain injury vary and affect each person differently. Examples of some effects include motor impairment (muscle weakness or paralysis, loss of coordination ability); dizziness and imbalance; fatigue and lack of motivation; chronic pain; visual and auditory problems; attention deficit; short- or long-term memory loss; difficulties in planning and problem solving; impulsivity; self-centered thinking with reduced ability for empathy; anger or depression; disinhibition, such as irresponsible behavior, inappropriate swearing, or sexual behavior; and communication problems.

I had a confronting experience relating to a person with an ABI. For 18 months I worked in a specific area of a major Australian city. Often I would stop at a particular petrol station and got to know the attendants very well. One young man, Ethan, was always ready with a smile and a joke. About eight months into my job, I was referred a person with an ABI. I entered the home and was shocked to find Ethan. He had sustained an ABI from head injuries received in a motorcycle accident. He was 22 years old. As a result of his ABI Ethan experienced depression, fatigue, and impulsivity. These traits affected his willingness and motivation to travel, as well as causing an inability to make consistently safe road crossing decisions. No amount of training, behavioral techniques, or reasoning were able to reduce his impulsivity, because the impulsivity resulted directly from the brain injury. Ethan's mobility goal had to take into account the effects of his medical condition. Therefore, the travel-training goal for Ethan was to walk from his home to the local corner shop to purchase items of his choice and return home. The route to the shop did not involve road crossing and took Ethan 15 minutes to walk. On the route, there were places for him to rest. Further, he carried a mobile phone to contact family members if he felt the need for emotional support. Travel-training occurred only when Ethan felt emotionally strong enough to do it. The travel-training goal was achieved because it took into account Ethan's medical condition. If the travel goal had been extended to include road crosses and public transport, then it would probably have been beyond Ethan's physical, cognitive, and emotional ability.

Learning disability

People with learning disabilities do not necessarily have an intellectual disability but experience difficulty perceiving, processing, analyzing, or remembering spatial, visual, or auditory information. Learning disability and IQ are not interrelated. Difficulty arises from a disruption in information processing. For example, when someone speaks to us, we need to recognize the words being spoken, interpret their meaning, decipher what relevance the meaning has to us, and remember the string of words as a sentence. Many of these complex functions occur in different parts of the brain and we need to link these processes together. It's little wonder these processes sometimes get mixed up.

Learning impairment sometimes becomes apparent in childhood when a child has difficulty reading, writing, speaking, communicating, or paying attention. Teachers might notice that a child struggles to complete work that should be easy for that child, or the child finds it difficult to follow directions for games or activities. A common verbal learning disability is dyslexia, which affects a person's ability to recognize and process letters and sounds of letters. A person with dyslexia will often have difficulty with reading and writing. Other people's ability to read or write might not be affected, but they might not be able to relate to the meaning of the words. For example, a child might read "the cat is on the mat" but be unable to form an understanding or a mental picture of the meaning of this sentence.

People with non-verbal learning disabilities might not be able to process or make sense of what they see. They might confuse letters, believing a "p" is a "q" or a plus is a minus sign. Other areas that might be affected include motor skills, visual-spatial skills, and interpersonal skills.

Trainers can use a number of strategies to teach a travel route to students who experience learning impairment. For example, the language used by the trainer needs to be succinct so that it can be more easily understood and transferred to short-term, then long-term memory. The travel-training goal can be reduced into small learning segments with a complete segment being learned before moving on to the next segment. Training instruction can be provided both in verbal and written form. I have found it effective to begin a session by succinctly describing what is going to be taught. With this, I have also provided some students who are literate with a written checklist of skills and activities included in the lesson which can be ticked off as we progress through training. At the conclusion of the session I also provide the student with a verbal summary and we discuss this content. Students are encouraged to review the checklist after training and bring it with them to the next training session. At the next session, we discuss the previous session's checklist and repeat the process of describing the skills and activities of the session, and a new checklist is provided for that session. I have found that presenting training sessions in this way encourages the student's organizational skills, self-reliance, and confidence. Importantly, each training session is given extra time if the student requires it.

Anxiety disorder

Anxiety disorders are medical conditions characterized by ongoing and excessive worry. The cause of anxiety disorders is largely unknown, though it is thought to be related to a combination of stressful life events, personality traits, and possibly biochemical changes. These disorders can take many forms and usually interfere with a person's ability to function or enjoy day-to-day pleasures. Usually the person feels that something dreadful is going to happen. Often anxiety is accompanied by levels of depression and can include such characteristics as compulsions and obsessions which cannot be controlled, consistent and excessive worry, intense worry in social situations, panic attacks, and an irrational fear of everyday objects or animals (e.g. cotton wool or birds). Physical reactions to anxiety often include an inability to sleep, breathing difficulties, stomach disorders, pounding heart, muscle tension, choking, feeling shaky or faint, dry mouth, numbness or tingling in the hands or feet, nausea, confusion, and excessive sweating.

Although students have presented at the commencement of travel-training with varying degrees of anxiety, they have usually received some intervention that has enabled them to function with their anxiety, such as medication or psychotherapy. But their anxiety must be taken into consideration when setting a travel-training goal. Appropriate considerations include:

- Teaching a short route that is of interest to the student. If they choose a route that is lengthy, then it is reduced into small segments and only one segment is taught at a time. For example, if a student wants to travel from home to a particular shop, then often teaching the last segment first provides positive feelings for the student. This is known as "backward chaining." This means you might first teach the student the route from only a block away from the shop so they are motivated by reaching the destination quickly.

- Routes that avoid objects or animals that make the student anxious (avoiding walking past a house with a barking dog in the front yard).

- Choosing a training time suitable for the student (they might prefer a time when it's quieter, with less traffic or pedestrians).

- Using a calm voice and providing lots of encouragement during training.

- Inviting them to include and practice their coping strategies during the route, such as mindfulness and deep breathing.

- Incorporating "safe places" into the route where they can go and gather their thoughts and practice their coping strategies privately (e.g. a quiet area or corner in a train station where they can turn their back on pedestrians).

Attention deficit hyperactivity disorder

ADHD is a disorder that affects children's behavior and is more commonly diagnosed in boys than girls. There is no correlation between ADHD and intelligence, although it does sometimes affect the student's ability to concentrate and learn. The three main difficulties children with ADHD experience are:

- inattention: difficulty concentrating, forgetfulness, not completing tasks before moving to another

- overactivity: constant restlessness and always being on the go

- impulsivity: talking over others and becoming quickly agitated.

Importantly, children with ADHD do not intend to be difficult and often find the condition frustrating and exhausting.

Although the exact causes of ADHD are unknown, there appears to be contributing factors such as genetics, exposure to lead which might influence brain chemistry, lack of early attachment, and neurophysiology, which includes differences in brain anatomy, metabolism, and electrical activity.

Despite the difficulties experienced by children with ADHD they can sometimes focus on activities they particularly enjoy. Channeling their excessive energy into sports, dancing, and other high-energy activities is advantageous as these are positive activities for which they can receive praise and acknowledgement, which helps build their self-esteem. When considering travel-training, the goal must not include high-risk activities such as road crossing or public transport. Instead, children can learn short walking routes where there are no driveways or road crossings, for example, from the car into the football club or from home to the local park. It's important that the trainer communicates calmly and clearly with the child, providing instructions at a physically close distance to gain the child's full attention. Providing only one or two instructions at a time and keeping the rules of travel clear and simple will help to keep the child focused. Providing lots of positive reinforcement will help keep the child motivated and engaged in learning.

Understanding your student is the first step before establishing the travel-training goal. In this way, you are providing the student with the greatest possible chance of success. The next step is to plan the route, then teach this route to your student.

KEY POINTS

» A travel-training goal is an intention with a specific beginning and end. For example: the student will walk from their classroom to the corner shop to purchase a drink.

» To establish a realistic and achievable goal, six major questions need to be answered:

- Has the student ever traveled independently?

- Where does the student need to travel?

- Is the student motivated to travel?

- Is the student emotionally ready for travel-training?

- Can the student cross roads independently?

- What medical aspects might affect travel-training?

4

Planning and Teaching a Travel Route

Once a realistic and achievable travel-training goal has been identified it is time to consider the processes and techniques of training.

As an example, 22-year-old Sam has an intellectual disability and is a reasonably experienced traveler who enjoys visiting bookshops. A new bookshop has opened at the local shopping mall and Sam is keen to learn how to get there. The route involves Sam walking to a bus stop near his home, traveling on a bus to the mall, and once at the mall walking to the bookshop. Some planning decisions need to be made before training commences.

Planning the route

First, we need to decide how frequent Sam's training sessions will be. As mentioned previously, travel-training needs to be as stress free as possible for both the student and trainer. It also needs to fit into the routine of family life without being too disruptive. It's ideal that training occurs only once or twice weekly so that Sam looks forward to traveling the route rather than it becoming a boring task.

Second, we need to decide who will teach Sam the route. It's preferable that only one or two trainers train him. Consistency in the training approach as well as the language used is very important, and often contributes to the program's success. The more trainers involved in a travel-training program, the less effective training will be.

Third, we need to divide the route into small segments to reduce the amount that Sam needs to learn in a session.

The outcome of these planning decisions is that primarily his mother, Beth, will teach Sam the route and when she is unavailable, his sister will take over. Training sessions will occur once a week on a day and time that suits both of them. They have decided to reduce the route to only three segments because Sam is a reasonably experienced traveler.

Sam is confident walking into a shop and seeking items, a skill he learned in his first travel-training route. He is able to enter the bookshop independently and does not need to be taught to do this. The segments of Sam's route will include:

1. walking from home to the bus stop

2. traveling on a bus to the mall

3. walking from the mall bus stop to the bookshop.

Which segment to teach first?

It's often advantageous to train the final segment of a route first of all (segment 3). This is called "backward chaining" and is described in Chapter 5. Therefore, on Sam's route he would first learn the walking route from the mall bus stop to the bookshop. The main reason for backward chaining is that it will keep Sam motivated and focused on learning the route as he will arrive at the bookshop in a short time to enjoy looking at the books. As the route is a lengthy one, his mother can drive him to the mall bus stop where training on this segment can commence. If Beth cannot drive him to this stop, then she has the option of walking with Sam to the bus stop near their home, traveling on the bus, and exiting at the mall bus stop. The actual travel-training, however, would only commence from the mall bus stop to the bookshop.

Once Sam has learned the last segment of the route, Beth can teach the next segment: traveling on the bus (segment 2). Once Sam has learned to travel on the bus, then the final segment can be taught, which involves walking from his home to the bus stop near his home (segment 1).

One of the advantages of backward chaining is that the student progressively builds skills and confidence while staying motivated because they reach their final goal (the bookshop) every time. This success helps keep everyone motivated to continue (Sam and the trainer). As well, the actual period of training is short, as Sam can already perform some segments independently and is being supported, rather than actively trained, by others.

How to teach route segments

The important techniques of training are:

- using lots of praise and positivity

- ignoring mistakes and redirecting the student's attention to the correct behavior

- only talking to the student to provide praise or to teach, and

- following the student's natural tendencies (see Chapter 5).

Let's apply these techniques to Sam's route to the bookshop. Use language during training that is casual, kind, non-threatening, and easily understood by your student.

Segment 3: Teaching Sam the route from the mall bus stop to the bookshop

Prior to training, Beth needs to plan the safest route from the bus stop to the bookshop. She needs to do this *without* Sam. Ideally, the safest route would be chosen, avoiding as many vehicles as possible and using major pedestrian paths rather than unsafe quiet back streets. Road crossings, if possible, need to occur at designated controlled crossings such as traffic lights or pedestrian crossings.

Once she has planned the route on her own, Beth might approach training in the following way:

1. Because she is only actively training Sam on segment 3, she may drive him to the mall bus stop, or catch the bus with him from home to the stop without actually training him on the earlier segments.

2. At the mall bus stop she will calmly inform Sam that they will walk the route to the bookshop together. She will also mention that she will not talk about anything else other than training because she wants him to just observe which way he is going. She will mention that if he wants to discuss anything else, then they can talk about it once they have reached the bookshop. Because Sam has never been to the bookshop, she will walk beside him while he observes which direction to go. If there are one or two significant landmarks on the way that might help Sam remember the direction, then she will also mention those as they pass them. A landmark is a unique object in the environment that is permanent, and serves as a marker (see glossary). For example, she might say, "We have to turn up this road—at this blue building." Where needed, Beth will include any landmarks she knows are important or meaningful to Sam as he is more likely to remember these: for example, "turn right at the yellow roast chicken shop" or "turn left at the car repair shop." It is important that Beth does not include too many landmarks as this might only confuse Sam.

   On the route to the bookshop there is a crossing at traffic lights. Beth knows that Sam is aware that he needs to press the button and wait for the signal to cross at the lights. When approaching the lights Beth remains quiet and stands back, waiting for Sam to press the button.

The point here is that if the student knows how to perform a skill then you do not need to jump in and teach it. Instead, stand back and let the student perform the skill. Provide only the minimum amount of assistance the student needs, in any one step.

If Sam forgets to press the button, then Beth might offer a simple prompt: "We're now at the traffic lights—what do you need to do?" She'll give Sam time to problem solve instead of telling him what to do. Once he presses the button at the traffic light, Beth simply provides praise, perhaps saying, "That's great Sam, you've pressed the button." The praise needs to be heartfelt and not too exaggerated. Beth needs to be real and honest in her praise, which will have a greater positive impact on Sam. If a student believes that you sincerely admire their behavior and are not just following a "script," then often they'll repeat the behavior. They'll realize that their behavior is significant and is a behavior that's respected.

When providing praise it is important that you identify the reason for your praise so that it has meaning to the student. In this case Beth has said it's terrific because Sam had *pressed the button*. It is difficult for students to repeat behavior if they do not understand exactly which behavior you are praising.

3. Once having crossed at the lights, Beth and Sam walk the remainder of the route to the bookshop. Beth walks silently, allowing Sam to observe and absorb whatever information he is taking in that helps him orient himself. If Sam talks about topics apart from training, Beth might kindly say, "Let's talk about that at the bookshop. I'm just watching where we're going at the moment." She'll smile and be kind, demonstrating ease and confidence.

4. Sam and Beth arrive at the bookshop. Previously, he has been taught to call Beth on his mobile phone whenever he arrives at his destination. To reinforce this and to build

the phone call into this current route, he must call her when he arrives at the bookshop even though she is standing nearby. Again, Beth congratulates Sam for traveling to the bookshop and for ringing her. If Sam attempted to talk about other topics apart from travel-training when walking to the bookshop, then now is the time for Beth to talk about the topics he raised. Sam is already familiar with entering shops independently. Sam and Beth agree that he will go into the bookshop and when finished, meet her outside the bookshop at a designated place (at a particular seat).

If Sam was not confident with entering the shop or purchasing an item he would need to learn these skills, and they would be built into the segments for this route (see Chapters 8 and 9).

How to fade out from this segment

"Fading out" means that Beth will start to move further away from Sam so that he can perform more of the segment independently. The question most frequently asked by trainers is "How do you know when it is time to start fading out?" The answer: when the student starts to perform part of the route independently and no longer needs you to be beside them to teach or provide praise. Once the student starts performing a part of the route independently then a "performance criterion" for fading out is set. A criterion is a measured and systematic way to fade out. A criterion is a specific number of times the trainer will observe the student perform a part of the route to ensure that they are actually performing that section reliably, consistently, and independently. Once the criterion has been achieved (e.g. the trainer observed the student performing the skill or part of the route successfully and consecutively five times), the trainer moves further away and sets another observation criterion. However, if during the five observations, the student makes an error then the skill is retrained and the criterion is reset from the first observation. This process continues until the trainer has completely faded out from the program.

For example, Sam and Beth might have walked the route a few times from the mall bus stop to the bookshop. Then Beth observed that Sam had started to walk across the controlled crossing without prompting, knew the direction to the bookshop, was happy to walk 8 meters (26 feet) in front of her, and happy to enter the bookshop by himself. This would be a great opportunity for Beth to commence fading out. At this point Beth might decide to observe Sam five times, consecutively, on these aspects. At the crossing she might say to Sam, "You've done so well. You keep walking ahead of me and I'll be behind you [at about 8 meters (26 feet)]. You go into the bookshop and I'll wait for you on the seat outside the bookshop." Sam appeared happy with this arrangement and continued to walk to the shop with Beth following 8 meters behind *without providing any assistance or praise*. They met at the usual seat when he had finished in the shop.

Sam successfully walked this segment of the route five times over five weeks, with no assistance or praise from Beth, and, therefore, met the five-time criterion. Sometimes during the observation period, unexpected events can occur. This is good! For instance, there might be a loud thunderstorm which disturbs Sam, or a stranger might approach him and start talking to him. The point here is that unexpected events often occur on a route. If the student has an adverse reaction to these then the trainer can teach them how to handle such situations if they are still following close by. However, if a trainer fades out from a route too quickly without an appropriate observation period and an incident occurs, then the trainer will have to return to the student from a great distance away or re-enter the route for retraining. This is demoralizing for both the trainer and student, with one or both feeling that training has failed.

The length of the observation period after the trainer believes the student is independent on a skill—or part of the route—depends on the level of risk on a particular segment. For example, if Sam had learned to cross a road, then the trainer might observe him doing this crossing approximately eight to ten times, depending on the complexity of the road and the number of cars traveling on it. In contrast, the trainer only needed to observe Sam a few times in the shop because there was no life-threatening danger.

Returning to Sam's route… Once he had satisfied the five-time observation criterion, Beth continued fading out from the program. Instead of waiting for him on the seat she moved further away to the entrance of the mall, about 40 meters (130 feet) away. At the traffic lights, she told Sam to keep walking to the bookshop and she would meet him near the mall entry when he had finished in the bookshop. He understood and agreed, and continued to the bookshop while she waited at the mall entry. When Sam was finished he met Beth at the mall entry. Beth set a criterion of three observations on this section of the route. However, if Sam had appeared nervous because Beth was waiting so far away, then she would have moved a little further into the mall, though of course not as close as the seat where she waited originally. Once she waited at the entry three times and believed Sam was confident, she decided to observe him from even further away, another three times.

Beth repeated this process of fading out in small steps until she was able to wait at the mall bus stop and say to Sam, "You walk to the bookshop and I'll meet you here when you finish." (When training a student on a route, this level of independence might take a little time to achieve. Time is irrelevant—as with all individualized training, it simply takes as long as it takes for a student to become independent. The student determines the timeframe for learning each skill or segment.)

Segment 2: Teaching Sam the bus route to the mall

Sam can now walk independently (i.e. unaccompanied) from the mall bus stop to the bookshop (segment 3). Beth is now required to teach segment 2, which includes traveling on a bus from home to the mall. Beth and Sam live close to the bus stop. They walk from home to the bus stop and training starts at the bus stop. Sam had previously learned the process of catching a bus. However, Beth still needs to train Sam on aspects particular to this bus stop.

For example, she teaches him exactly where to stand to wait for his bus near the bus stop sign. If Sam was sitting down or standing too far from the sign, then the driver might not see him and drive by. Sam also needs to identify the bus number. He refers to a cue card kept in his wallet upon which the bus number is written. When he arrives at the bus stop, he takes out his cue card and his money, ready to buy his ticket. Sam has learned to compare the number on the cue card with the number displayed on the bus and can identify his bus. When he sees it coming Sam waves to the driver alerting him to stop so that he can board. Once inside, Sam purchases his ticket and takes a seat as close as possible to the front of the bus so that he can see where he is going, be close to the driver if he requires assistance, and avoid crowds when he exits the bus. If seats are available, Sam can be encouraged to sit on the same side as the door so he will see when he is close to the mall bus stop. During training, Beth will teach Sam to ring the bell (to alert the driver that he wants to exit the bus at the next bus stop) at a particular landmark. Ideally, the landmark is chosen by Sam, as this will increase the chance of him remembering it. Sam chose to ring the bell when the bus traveled past a service station, since the large yellow shell above the service station appealed to him. Once the bus drove past the sign, Sam was taught to ring the bell immediately. When the bus stopped at the mall bus stop, Sam exited the bus. Because he previously learned the walking route from this bus stop to the mall bookshop (segment 3), Beth allows him to walk the rest of the way to the bookshop independently.

Similar to the segment taught first (segment 3), Beth fades out slowly from the bus segment to ensure Sam has the skills to travel on the bus independently. That is:

- Sam rings the bell at the service station, over five consecutive trips, without prompts (with Beth sitting next to him).

- Sam rings the bell over two consecutive trips, without prompts (with Beth sitting three seats away from him toward the back of the bus).

- Sam rings the bell over two consecutive trips, without prompts (with Beth sitting another five seats away from him toward the back of the bus).

- Sam rings the bell over five consecutive trips, without prompts (with Beth sitting at the back of the bus).

Because the process of fading out had been gradual, Beth observed Sam ring the bell and exit the bus 14 times without prompts. Once she had made the final observations at the back of the bus, she allowed Sam to travel on the bus independently (i.e. on his own). Beth followed the bus in her car to observe him ten times, although she could have also driven ahead of the bus to meet him at the mall bus stop. Once Beth had observed Sam travel the bus from her car successfully ten consecutive times, then Sam was considered independent and could now travel on the bus (segment 2) and walk to the mall bookshop by himself (segment 3).

Segment 1: Teaching Sam the walking route from home to the bus stop

The bus stop was approximately 500 meters (1640 feet) from Sam's home and there were no road crosses on the way. Beth followed the same training procedure as in the other two segments. She and Sam left their home and walked to the bus stop. When Beth believed Sam knew the direction to the bus stop, she faded out in the following way.

- Sam walked the route to the bus stop twice without error with Beth walking 4 meters (13 feet) behind him.

- Sam walked the route to the bus stop twice without error with Beth walking further behind him at 20 meters (65 feet).

- Sam walked the route to the bus stop once without error with Beth following at 40 meters (130 feet).

- Sam walked the route to the bus stop twice without error while Beth observed him from the other side of the road, without him realizing she was there.

Sam was then considered independent and could now travel to the mall bookshop by himself.

Sequencing travel-training skills

I recommend that, once a beginner traveler has learned to travel a route independently, they continue to travel that route for at least three months before they are taught another route. Teaching an additional route too early may be overwhelming or confusing for the student. Just allow them time to absorb and be completely comfortable with what they have already learned: this will help to increase the student's self-confidence as well as the confidence of their family or others involved in their life. Ideally, teach at least one or two routes at the beginner level before introducing intermediate-level travel-training. The skills at the beginner level must include vehicle awareness; how to contact a significant person to alert them of their arrival at their destination; and how to seek assistance from "safe" members of the community. Other skills that are taught depend on the individual's need, such as learning the "avoid dog" strategy (see Chapter 6) or coping strategies to deal with noise or crowds.

Once the student has learned these foundation skills, they can continue to learn routes that include road crossing. Ideally, teach only one type of road crossing at a time, beginning with crossing at traffic lights. Only move on to teach more complex road crossing types when the student is crossing independently at lights. Road crossing is complex and each type of road crossing must be approached using a different strategy. For instance, the rules to cross at traffic lights are very different from the rules to cross at pedestrian crossings or uncontrolled crossings. Start teaching at traffic lights, then pedestrian crossings, and finally, small uncontrolled road crossings that have fewer cars driving on them.

KEY POINTS

» Before starting to teach a route, plan it carefully by traveling the route without the student.

» Some important planning decisions include: identifying the trainer (one to two trainers only); the frequency of training (one to two times per week maximum); the day and time training will occur; the number of teaching segments the route will comprise; relevant cues or landmarks; and whether or not to backward chain the route.

» The essential techniques of training include: using lots of praise and positivity; ignoring mistakes and redirecting the student to the correct behavior; only talking with the student to provide praise or to teach; and following the student's natural tendencies.

» Fade out from the route slowly to ensure the student has the skills to travel it safely and independently.

» Beginner travelers learn skills such as independent walking (no road crosses), in-shop purchase of one to two items, how to use a mobile phone, and how to seek assistance.

» Intermediate travelers learn skills such as walking routes with controlled crossings (e.g. traffic light crossings and, later, pedestrian crossings) and then uncontrolled crossings.

» Advanced travelers learn longer routes, possibly using buses, trains, and other forms of public transport.

» Essentially, travel-training is teaching skills that slowly increase in complexity according to the student's travel goal, and fading out only once the performance criteria have been reached.

Part 3

TRAVEL-TRAINING
IMPORTANT
CONSIDERATIONS

"When I let go of what I am,
I become what I might be."

Lao Tzu

5

Techniques for Travel-Training

Teaching a student the skills of travel-training requires the trainer to have a number of effective teaching strategies to draw upon. Some strategies that I've used and adapted originate from the work of the American behavioral psychologist Burrhus Frederic Skinner. Skinner's techniques help to modify behavior. Essentially, Skinner believed that when an individual responds to events in the environment (for example, checking at a roadside to see there are no cars, then commencing to cross the road) and the individual is praised by the trainer for correctly judging and crossing the road ("Well done John. There are no cars and you are walking across the road") then that behavior of road crossing will continue to occur over time because of the trainer's positive response. The important element in this example is the provision of positive reinforcement *immediately after* the student has responded correctly. The immediate delivery of positive reinforcement to a correct behavior strengthens that behavior. Skinner's model included various training methods such as shaping, modeling, prompting, fading and more—all of which I will explain in more detail.

First, though, it is important to acknowledge that while Skinner's model of training is powerful, it is by no means perfect. Each person is an individual experiencing conscious and unconscious cognitive processes, and with varying biology that can also affect behavior.

I have seen this variation in people while travel-training time and time again. For example, I was at a follow-up consultation with a parent whose daughter, Ingrid, begrudgingly wore a red hat to increase her visibility and safety when traveling. The mother explained that she had provided a lot of positive reinforcement (praise) when her daughter put the hat on and wore it throughout training. But when the mother and I observed Ingrid walking the route from home to the shopping center where she would buy her lunch—an activity she loved—she took the hat off, carried it, and dropped it many times (deliberately?). So, despite applying the correct training technique of positive reinforcement, it did not work for Ingrid. Why? Because human beings are complex and we do not fully understand the reason for all behavior. Perhaps Ingrid didn't enjoy the feeling of the hat on her head; perhaps she felt silly wearing a hat; perhaps the hat made her feel hot; perhaps she didn't even know why she disliked the hat—there could be a million reasons. The fact remained that she was not going to wear that red hat: there was no reinforcer strong enough to tempt her to wear it. And that is fine. The point is, it's the individual's preference and choice that determines the approach a trainer takes.

This lesson highlights that during training it is sometimes necessary to "go with the flow" of an individual's nature. I suggested to the mother that there were other options for increasing Ingrid's visibility and safety when traveling. Instead of a red hat, she could wear a red or yellow shirt, or an orange scarf, or a carry a red backpack. Simply, she could wear any item(s) she liked in bright red, yellow, or orange above the waist so that vehicle drivers could easily see her.

A day after this conversation, I had an excited phone call from the mother. Before they walked to the shopping center that afternoon, Ingrid chose to wear her favorite yellow dress. Also, upon learning she didn't need to wear the red hat anymore, she laughed, ran into her bedroom and threw the hat under her bed— probably never to be retrieved again.

Following are some effective training techniques that you can apply when travel-training your student.

Reinforcement—let's be positive!

Reinforcement (e.g. verbal praise) is a response to a particular behavior that will most likely increase that behavior. Therefore, only provide positive reinforcement to behaviors or skills you want to happen more often, or in a particular situation. When a student is learning a task, it is important to give praise *immediately after* the behavior you want has occurred. For example, when Jess rings the bus bell to exit the bus you might say a moment later, "Well done Jess. That's terrific! You've rung the bell." Because you have immediately praised her and told her why you praised her (for ringing the bus bell at the right place), it is likely she will ring the bell again in future. It is important to provide praise *immediately after* the correct response so that the person knows exactly which behavior you are praising.

There are many types of positive reinforcers, and you must understand the individual you are training so that you provide reinforcers that are meaningful and motivating to that person. For example, some students respond positively to verbal praise ("Well done Jess. You've rung the bus bell"). Others respond to hand signals such as a "thumbs up," which means "Well done." You might also like to offer your student a "secondary reinforcer" after they have completed a successful training session, such as doing an activity they love (e.g. playing on the computer or going to the park to play). In this situation, as well as praising your student immediately after they ring the bus bell or purchase a train ticket correctly, the student can engage in a favorite activity post-training ("After you ring the bus bell, Phillip, and we get off the bus, you can go home and play a computer game").

Some students respond positively to "tokens" (e.g. small plastic disks) once they understand the meaning of them. For example, a student might enjoy going to the beach. In this case, at home on a wall chart, iPad, or equivalent, you might display a photo of his favorite beach and explain that when he puts his backpack on to walk to the shop (or whatever the desired behavior is) he will receive one token. When the student performs the correct behavior and puts on the backpack independently, give him a token to apply to his wall chart goal. There might be five spaces for five tokens on the chart—when the child has earnt five tokens (by putting his backpack on independently over five training sessions) he receives the reward of going to his favorite beach. Please do not set an overly large number of tokens which a student must earn before he can receive a treat. This will only have the effect of demotivating the child and training will become a negative and discouraging experience. Remember, travel-training is supposed to be achievable and enjoyable for the student.

Types of reinforcement

As students gradually become independent on a task, they no longer need continuous reinforcement. This is similar to us. For example, when learning a new skill such as playing tennis we begin to learn how to hit the tennis ball. At first, our coach might give us continuous encouragement and praise us when we hit each ball. However, when we become more consistent at hitting the ball she might occasionally give us praise (if we hit a particularly good shot). We would probably think the coach was a bit strange if she continued to praise every ball we hit for months, and would tire of this pretty quickly. It's exactly the same for our students. We need to provide the amount of praise that is suitable to their stage of learning. Following are two commonly used types of reinforcement.

Reinforcement for the early stages of learning

Trainers provide "continuous reinforcement" to students during the *early stages* of learning a skill. That is, we reinforce a behavior such as crossing the road by praising the student *every single time* they make a correct road crossing decision. This continuous reinforcement of behavior communicates to the student that crossing the road correctly (or whatever skill you are teaching them) is the right behavior and to keep doing it.

Once the student begins to initiate crossing the road correctly we can move to a partial reinforcement approach.

Reinforcement as the student starts to use a new skill

Once the student begins to initiate crossing the road correctly, they do not need continuous praise. Instead, we provide reinforcement or praise *only part of the time.* I recommend providing reinforcement or praise after two or more correct responses. It might be that the student is walking a route that involves four road crosses. Rather than praising them every time, I might wait until the second road cross to say, "Well done. You crossed the road safely." Next time I might say at the fourth road crossing, "Well done. You crossed the road safely." Make the timing of your praise unpredictable: maybe the first time, then the sixth time, then the third time, and so on. Partial reinforcement communicates to the student that you trust their response and are pleased with them. Your intermittent praise helps maintain the student's confidence in performing the behavior and also encourages them to keep doing it so they receive your praise. After some time, the student will appear to be self-confident, and will perform the skill whenever it's needed.

When a student appears self-confident (evident by continuing to perform a skill correctly) you can slowly reduce the praise till you are no longer praising them. Praise is no longer required as they are independent on the skill. Generally, the student is reinforced naturally, just by being able to travel on the bus by themselves and reaching their desired destination.

Ignoring incorrect behavior

There are two basic rules I follow when travel-training a student. They are:

- Give positive reinforcement when the student is doing well and performing the desired behavior, and

- Ignore the behavior that I do not want continued.

For example, when a student is walking ahead of me but keeps looking back and talking to me, instead of saying, "Tom—stop talking and keep going," I avoid looking at him and ignore him.

Ignoring him means I am not reinforcing his talking by responding to him, which might keep his talking behavior going.

I do, however, ask myself why he is engaging in this behavior. Maybe he needs something I am not providing? Maybe he just loves attention and talking, in which case I might say before the lesson, "When we arrive at the shop we can have a chat about your day, but when you are walking I just want us to be quiet and keep walking." Or he might be fearful about walking so far ahead, in which case I'll walk a little closer to him and provide him with positive reinforcement to boost his confidence, such as, "That's great walking ahead Tom—just terrific."

In some instances when training, I will ignore an incorrect behavior and immediately divert the student to the correct behavior. For instance, if I am teaching a student to cross a road and they make an incorrect decision and attempt to walk onto the road when a car is coming, I gently block them with my hand. I might point to the oncoming car and say, "Car." I do not need to say anything negative, such as, "No. Stop. That's wrong." These negative comments teach very little and only decrease the student's confidence. In the moment of my refocusing their attention onto the car, they have observed on some level that they have made an incorrect decision and have received the lesson that "I do not walk when a car is coming."

Prompting

When we are teaching a skill such as taking money out of a wallet when purchasing an item at the shop, we need to provide guidance so that the student can eventually take the money of out of their wallet independently, at the right time, and without hesitating. Generally, at the beginning of teaching a skill we teach each step the same way many times over by showing the student what to do until they begin to initiate some parts of the skill. For example, the student might have learned to walk into the shop, choose a drink from the fridge, walk to the counter to pay, and take their wallet out of their bag. But then they might pause for a period of time and not move to the next step of opening the wallet to take out their money. It's at this moment that prompts are used to assist the student to proceed to the next step of taking the money out of their wallet. We can guide or prompt them in a variety of ways that include the following.

Verbal prompts

We might say to our student, Phil, "Good. You have your wallet— what do you need to do now?" If this prompt isn't enough to remind Phil to take his money out then he needs more directive prompting. You might then say, "Good. You have your wallet out—you need to take your money out now." These prompts will assist Phil in continuing to learn the process of paying for his item.

Physical guidance (sometimes called "shaping")

Physical guidance involves the trainer moving Phil's hand to the money in the wallet and helping him take out the money. However, this method is more intrusive, so Phil would need to feel comfortable with it. Some students do not like being touched or directed in this way, in which case this would be an unsuitable form of prompting. There is another method of physical guidance called "hand-under-hand shaping," which is less intrusive for students. For example, you might put your hand *under* your student's hand and move toward the wallet, cueing them to take out the money. With this method the student has the choice to either go with the trainer's hand or take their hand away, and is, therefore, more in control.

Modeling prompts (sometimes called "demonstration")

Modeling means the trainer demonstrates how to take the money out of the wallet so that Phil can see what he needs to do. After modeling what to do, the trainer returns the money to the wallet and presents it to Phil so that he can now try to take out the money.

If modeling is an effective way for your student to learn, then you might like to also use video modeling. Video modeling shows the student taped sequences of a desired behavior. For instance, a case manager who was to train a student to walk a route to work filmed a colleague walking the exact route while wearing a red hat and looking for traffic before crossing various roads. The case manager then showed the film to the student and they discussed important aspects of the route. The film helped the student to understand how to walk the route and was a reference point when being travel-trained: "Remember how [the colleague] pressed the button at the traffic lights in the video—well you can now do that too..."

Visual cues

If the trainer was to provide a visual cue to prompt Phil to take his money from his wallet, they might tap the wallet or point to the money in it, which might be enough to remind Phil of the next step in the sequence.

An important consideration when using prompts is to consider which of the prompts is the least intrusive that will still lead the student to do the next step in the task (or route). That is, if the student only needs a subtle visual cue (such as nodding toward their wallet), then do not use the other more intrusive cues. Remember, the goal is for the student to become independent in a skill, and the trainer eventually needs to remove themselves from the student. This is much harder to do if the student becomes reliant on a trainer's verbal or physical prompting and modeling.

Stop talking

When working with a student on a travel-training route there are only two occasions when the trainer needs to talk to that student (so as to not distract the student): first, to provide praise when the student has performed well and second, to teach a skill. At all other times the trainer is to be quiet.

To illustrate, the trainer might be at a bus stop teaching a student how to wave down a bus. While they wait for the bus they should not talk. Being quiet has the advantage of the student observing their environment rather than attending to the trainer. In these moments, students also have the opportunity to observe how others behave in public (good role-modeling) and learn to be in their own thoughts (they will need to be used to their own company when traveling independently). It also gives the trainer an opportunity to observe the appropriateness of the student's behavior. That is, does the student talk loudly to themselves; do they stand quietly and look in the direction that the bus will come; do they keep standing in the right position so that the bus driver will see them or do they move around? These observations will give the trainer insight into any additional skills that might need to be taught in preparation for independent bus travel.

If a student is used to the trainer talking to them, then the trainer might need to explain their own change in behavior. The trainer might need to say, "We're travel-training now at the bus stop. We need to concentrate and we're not going to chat about school until you're on the bus." Always let the student know what is happening to reduce any confusion they might feel.

Criteria setting and fading out from a program

This next story illustrates very clearly the importance of setting performance criteria for a student on a particular task before fading out (fading out is the gradual withdrawal of the trainer from a travel-training program). A young man, Murat, with an intellectual disability was traveling on a train. He had undertaken three weeks of training to learn how to board the train and to identify his destination. Once the trainer observed that Murat seemed to no longer need instruction on the train, he allowed Murat to travel the next week by himself on week four. While Murat was traveling by himself, the train stopped in the middle of the railway tracks, nowhere near a station. The train stood there for about ten minutes. There was no announcement explaining why it had stopped, which was confusing for passengers. Murat was standing near the train door which could be opened manually. He became impatient, opened the door, and climbed down onto the railway tracks. Thankfully no trains were passing at the time and he walked to safety. However, the question remains: how might this scenario have been prevented?

Clearly, Murat had learned lots of skills that enabled him to travel on the train. However, the trainer had overlooked a very important component of travel-training: namely, setting performance criteria before fading out.

The process of training a student is fairly straightforward. For example, when teaching a student to press the button at traffic lights, the teacher repetitively teaches pressing the button until the student starts to initiate pressing the button, and keeps training the student until they consistently press the button without requiring assistance or prompts of any kind. However, even though the student has learned to press the button without assistance or prompts, this does not mean they will press the button when the trainer is not there, or if someone begins talking to them at the traffic lights and distracts them. To "safety-proof" a student after they appear to know how to perform a skill, their skill must be tested under as many circumstances as possible. Trainers cannot conclude that, even though the student has performed the skill a few times, they will continue to do so reliably. This must be tested by setting a performance criterion.

In the case of Murat, let's apply criteria setting and fading out.

1. Once it became evident that Murat was able to consistently exit the train at the correct station, the trainer should then have commenced fading out as it appeared that Murat was traveling competently.

2. To fade out the trainer would sit a small distance away from Murat to see that he continued to exit the train at the correct station. The trainer would still be in sight of

Murat, and might set a criterion of five times: for example, on five consecutive journeys Murat will successfully and independently exit the train at the correct station.

3. When Murat satisfied this criterion, the trainer would continue to set criteria and fade out, gradually moving further back in the train.

4. Following this pattern of setting a criterion and fading out, the trainer would eventually fade out into other train compartments. He might be able to observe Murat, but Murat would not see the trainer, and would believe he was not being observed on the train.

5. Eventually, the trainer would have observed Murat travel on the train a number of times over a month or two. If there were no incidents during this period then the trainer could observe Murat from the exit station without having to travel on the train. At this point, the trainer might set the final criterion to observe Murat exit the train another three times before concluding he was independent on this route.

The benefit of fading out according to performance criteria is that it gives the trainer the opportunity to observe a student over a long period of time where incidents might occur. For example, the train might have stopped at a station for a longer period of time than usual where Murat might have become impatient and left the train at the wrong station; another person might have approached him and started a conversation; he might have been teased by school children; or he might have fallen asleep and missed his train stop. All of these incidents would have been training opportunities to teach Murat strategies to cope in these situations.

The level of a criterion is up to the discretion of the trainer. I tend toward safety and prefer a higher criterion in high-risk situations. For example, traveling on public transport is complex and the student is potentially exposed to a number of risky situations (as in Murat's case). Therefore, I would set a higher criterion so that I could observe the student for a longer period of time. Similarly, on road crossings, if the student is learning to cross busy roads then I would set a higher criterion than at a small crossing where there are fewer cars.

Teaching schedules

An important aspect of travel-training is that the student enjoys the experience and remains engaged and motivated to travel. Often, students do not even realize they are being trained, but are simply on their way to an enjoyable activity. I often recommend that a trainer teach travel-training no more than once a week. Any more frequently than this runs the risk of losing the student's interest. Of course there are always exceptions. If a student is highly motivated, is very keen to travel, and can cope with the demands of traveling more than once a week, then that is fine. The primary considerations are that the student remains motivated, and that learning is taking place.

Forward and backward chaining

If we think of a chain, it is a series of links joined together. One link depends on the other for the chain to exist. This is similar to the series of steps that need to be learned in any travel-training route. Each segment of the route is a link and the entire route is the chain.

"Forward" and "backward" chaining describes two sequences in which we might teach a route to a student. First, I would reduce the travel route into segments that I believe the student was capable of learning. For example, if my student, Jen, was learning her first independent route without road crosses from school to home I might break the route into the following small segments:

1. Exit school and walk 150 meters (500 feet) to Stern Street.

2. At the corner of Stern Street, turn right and walk to the corner of Berkeley Street.

3. At the corner of Berkeley Street turn left and walk the 50 meters (160 feet) home.

Next, I would consider which of the two chaining approaches I would use with Jen. I would take into account that this is Jen's first travel-training route and she has never walked anywhere independently, she lacks self-confidence, and she feels tired in the afternoon. I would, therefore, decide to "backward chain" this route. Backward chaining means that Jen would quickly understand that the purpose of the route is to get home. She loves being at home so this is a very rewarding route that helps to keep her motivated.

Backward chaining means I would teach the last segment (segment 3) first (that is, from the corner of Berkeley Street, turn left, and walk the 50 meters home). So, I would simply walk with Jen from school to the corner of Berkeley Street and then commence training. Once Jen was able to walk this section of the route independently (after I had tested this by setting criteria and slowly fading out), then I would teach segment 2 (from the corner of Stern Street, turn right and walk to the corner of Berkeley Street). This means I would then walk with Jen from school to the corner of Stern Street and commence training segment 2. As Jen is now independent on segment 3, when we finished the training session on segment 2, she would walk the rest of the way home independently. Once Jen was independent on segment 2, I would finally teach segment 1 (exit the school and walk 150 meters to Stern Street). When we completed training for the day on segment 1, she would walk the rest of the route home independently as she has learned segments 2 and 3. When she finally learned to travel segment 1 independently, she could walk from school to home independently.

In contrast, forward chaining means that I would have taught Jen this route from segment 1 to segment 3 in a "forward" chained sequence. That is, I would have first taught Jen to exit school and walk 150 meters to Stern Street independently. After each travel-training session I would have walked with Jen through segments 2 and 3 to her home without directly teaching her but role-modeling the correct way to walk. She might observe my behavior along the way or she might not—it does not matter. Once she was independent on segment 1, I would say to her, "Okay Jen, you walk to the corner of Stern Street (the beginning of segment 2) and I will meet you there." I would then walk to the corner of Stern Street without her seeing me and wait for her. We would commence training segment 2. Once she was independent on segment 2, which might take a number of weeks, I would say to Jen, "Great Jen. You walk to the corner of Berkeley Street and I will meet you there." Again, I would walk there without Jen seeing me, after which we would commence training on segment 3. Once she was independent on segment 3, I would say to her at the end of her school day, "Right, Jen. Now you can walk home…" She is now independent walking from school to home. The disadvantage of forward chaining this route is that Jen would have had to train on segment 1 before going home and it might have frustrated her that she was not walking directly home.

How do you choose which chaining approach to use with your student? Generally, if it is a lengthy or complex route or your student is not an experienced or confident traveler, then you would backward chain the route. You want the student to understand why they are learning the route, and reaching their destination quickly will help to cement their understanding. Second, you want to maintain the student's motivation to learn the route, so you need to make it easy for them to succeed.

For example, if you wanted to teach a student to travel to school in the early morning it could be demotivating to use forward chaining. Why? Because to begin with, many students resent getting out of bed and leaving home early in the morning. Then trying to focus them on training on a short segment from home, after which you must either walk with them the rest of the way to school or return home and then drive them to school might be frustrating and confusing. They are doing an activity that might seem pointless, too early in the morning, that seems unrelated to travelling to school. Instead, you could backward chain the route and either walk or drive the student to the last segment near the school and teach that segment of the route first—finishing at school. The benefit of backward chaining in this case is that they are near school so they understand the point of training immediately—to get to school.

Backward chaining is naturally motivating because the student reaches their end goal independently in the shortest amount of time. Essentially, make it easy for your students to succeed and do not overwhelm them with information or expectation.

KEY POINTS

» In the early stages of learning provide positive reinforcement (e.g. praise) *immediately after* your student has performed a skill successfully.

» As a student becomes increasingly competent at a travel-training skill, reduce the amount and regularity of praise.

» Ignore incorrect behavior, and praise the correct/ desired behavior.

» To assist learning, use a variety of prompts such as verbal, physical, visual, or modeling.

» Once you believe your student has learned a travel-training skill, test if this is actually the case by setting performance criteria and fading out slowly from the travel-training program.

» Deciding whether to forward or backward chain a travel-training program depends on the current skill level and motivation of your student as well as the complexity of the route.

6

Environmental Factors

One of the most important aspects of traveling independently for all of us is taking responsibility for our own safety and feelings of well-being. Travel-training teaches students to do just that. Following are some common issues that students face when traveling and some effective solutions to these problems.

Where's my red hat? Being visible to traffic

If you think about road conditions on any one day, there are a variety of factors that can reduce a pedestrian's visibility to traffic. For example, early in the morning or late in the afternoon, the sun can be shining in the driver's eyes; it might be dark, overcast, or raining; or there could be shadows cast from trees that decrease the visibility of pedestrians or pedestrian crossings. Drivers can also be tired, misinterpret road signals, or make mistakes when driving. However, pedestrians wearing bright colors can increase their safety as they are more easily seen by other pedestrians and drivers. The three best colors that increase a person's visibility are bright red, bright yellow, and bright orange (the "safety colors"). These colors stand out from the environment. For example, your student can wear a bright red cap, or carry a yellow bag, or wear an orange item of clothing such as a scarf or shirt. The bright color is most effective when worn above the waist as it is more easily seen by drivers. When a person crosses the road and is wearing an item of clothing or carrying a bag in one of these bright safety colors, the probability of drivers seeing the pedestrian is very high indeed.

Over the years I have worked in many schools with students and teachers. It is fantastic to see that, prior to exiting the school, each student goes and puts a red or yellow hat on as a matter of routine! At the child's home I recommend that a hat is left in a prominent place such as by the front door of the house or near their bedroom door. This serves as a reminder for the child to put the hat on before leaving home.

A red hat is also useful when your child is walking to and from school. If a red hat is not part of the school uniform, then the child can wear the hat from home to the school gate, then take it off and put it in their bag before walking into school. Most school principals are very happy with this practice when the benefits are explained to them. Some principals have even made it mandatory for all students to wear red hats to and from school. When commencing travel-training with your students, include one of these safety colors in their outfit so that it becomes part of the "leaving home" or "leaving school" routine.

Fear of dogs, loud noises, and people

Dogs

It is not uncommon for students to run the opposite way, even onto the road, when they see a dog walking toward them. Often, the student is experiencing so much fear that they do not know what they are doing, where they are running, or the consequence of their action. When the student starts running, often the dog thinks they are playing and runs after them, which can be a terrifying experience for the student.

However, with training, students can be taught the following "avoid dog" strategy which has proven to be very successful. When the student sees a dog coming toward them, they stop and bend their elbows and put both hands on their upper chest near the shoulders. This action will prevent their arms from flailing around, which can attract the dog, who might think it is the beginning of a game. Next, the student turns their back to the dog, though they turn their head slightly to keep their eyes on the dog as it passes by. As the dog walks toward them, then next to them, then past them, the student keeps their back to the dog. When the dog has passed, the student continues on their way. This action communicates to the dog that the student is not interested in any type of contact or play. Therefore, there is little reason for the dog to approach the student or stay in their presence for any length of time.

Teaching a student to take this action requires shaping and modeling. For example, remembering that the student is experiencing great fear, explain each step of the procedure and assist them to take these actions. You might help them place their hands on their upper chest or you might model this behavior, explaining that this tells the dog that you do not want to play. Gently place your hands on the student's shoulders or do whatever you need to do to reassure the student they are safe with you and all will be okay. As the dog walks by, assist the student to keep their back to the dog until the dog has passed. Finally, reinforce and praise the student that they did very well and walk on. Repeat the procedure as needed until the student can demonstrate this behavior confidently when a dog approaches.

Loud noise

For a variety of reasons, some students cannot stand the sound of loud noise. Loud noise might include police sirens, thunder, the cries of babies, music, or the noise of crowds. Regardless of the source of the loud noise, age-appropriate strategies can be used to "mask" the noise so that it can be tolerated by the student. Some successful strategies include:

- Listening to music via earplugs. I have used this strategy often with students traveling on public transport or during thunderstorms. Listening to music often masks the loud noise to some degree but, importantly, focuses the person's attention onto the music rather than on the noise.

- Inserting earplugs (in-ear headphones) when detecting loud noise. This is particularly useful for older students when traveling in public. Some earplugs block incoming sound waves when they detect noise over a given threshold. When the noise stops, the earplugs allow the hearer to hear at a normal range again. Earplugs can be skin color and blend into the ear, making them virtually undetectable to others. Try before you buy and test that the seal is both tight and comfortable.

- Noise-cancelling headphones which cover the entire ear ("over-ear headphones") and have the added advantage of being comfortable to wear for longer periods of time.

- Blocking the ears with the fingers. This simple strategy is useful particularly when passing loud noise from crowds, drilling, or machinery used on work sites.

- Locating a quiet area. For some students, loud noise can be so intrusive and disruptive that they need to find a quiet place (perhaps inside a shop or office, or in a quiet area outdoors) where they can simply cover their ears, and close their eyes to separate themselves from the disruption. This strategy is particularly useful when the loud noise will subside quickly, such as an ambulance siren or a loud motorbike.

Build these techniques into your travel-training sessions for students who are sensitive to noise.

People

Sometimes students experience anxiety when entering a place where there are crowds (e.g. a party or a railway platform) or people they know (e.g. a family gathering). However, once they have entered the environment and undertake an activity, the anxiety can pass or be managed by the students.

Age-appropriate strategies to manage anxiety can be beneficial for the students to help them avoid unwanted attention. There is evidence from individuals with autism that adapted cognitive behavior therapy (CBT) can be effective for some students. CBT adaptations that seem to reduce anxiety include the student engaging in hands-on tasks (e.g. playing a game on their mobile phone while waiting for public transport), a trainer using pictorial stories to explain how to cope in a social situation that the student might find themselves in, and incorporating an individual's interests when entering an anxiety-producing situation (e.g. taking a magazine to read when traveling).

In addition to CBT, some successful strategies to reduce social anxiety include:

- listening to music via earphones

- a parent/adult telling a story in advance, for example, about a party the student might need to attend, which includes scenarios about what might happen at the party, and what the student can do while at the party to help them feel relaxed

- teaching the student to walk into a gathering, say hello, smile, and keep walking until they arrive at a safe place in the house (e.g. a quiet room where they can read or play a game).

Avoid strategies that draw attention to the student, such as walking into a gathering or public place with their head covered with a blanket, or forcing a student to enter a gathering or public place without any strategy. An effective anxiety-reducing strategy takes into account the individual's strengths and interests—build on those creatively.

Stranger danger

An important part of travel-training is teaching "stranger danger": that is, teaching students to be safe, to be aware of predatory strangers, and to protect themselves. A stranger is anyone that your student does not know. This person can be male or female, of any age, and dressed in any way.

Teaching stranger danger is a process of raising awareness, without unnecessarily alarming the student. There are some basic rules you can teach, as well as role-model. These include:

- Never initiate conversation with a stranger.

- Never get into a car with a person that they don't know.

- Always walk or travel straight to a destination with a sense of purpose.

- Avoid walking or traveling through places where there are few people, and keep to well-lit areas at night.

- Do not accept gifts/rewards of any type from strangers.

- If a stranger in a car stops to talk, walk away quickly, yell for help, or walk into a shop or house to get help.

- Seek help from a shopkeeper, railway guard, bus driver, or a police person if they feel scared.

- Use the mobile phone to ring a trusted person.

- Ignore strangers who make up sad stories such as needing help to look for a lost pet or child, or needing directions.

Sometimes parents of older children express frustration that despite these "rules" their child still talks to strangers. In these situations you might:

- Have the child listen to music via their personal music device while traveling on public transport. Any activity that appeals to the child can be used to distract them from talking to others.

- Reinforce that the child sits as close as possible to the driver. In this way, the driver is alerted to any unusual activity and the chance of someone interfering in a negative way with the child is reduced.

Often, "natural consequences" can teach an older student appropriate behavior. If the student initiates conversation with a stranger, then the stranger will react either positively or negatively. I have seen adults engage in conversation with the student on a bus or train for a period of time, and then when the adult tires, they either ignore the student or ask them to be quiet. I have also seen adults get angry with a talkative student. Mostly, this affects the student's behavior. Sometimes they become quiet, or move away. Importantly, these situations are learning experiences for the student and, as a result, they often become hesitant to engage with adults who are unknown to them.

Encourage the student to tell

If students do encounter a stranger, then encourage them to tell you about the incident. You can do this by including this encouragement in your initial training about stranger danger. For example, reinforce the message that "If a stranger talks to you, or you feel unsure or uncomfortable around a stranger then it would be great if you come and tell me about it." If the student tells you about an incident, then you must listen openly and praise them for telling you. There are also illustrated books and e-books available to assist you in communicating stranger danger strategies to your student.

KEY POINTS

» Have your student carry a bag or wear an item of clothing from the waist up in bright red, bright yellow, or bright orange to increase their visibility and safety when traveling (e.g. orange bag, or a red hat, or a yellow shirt).

» If your student is frightened of dogs, teach them the "avoid dog" strategy.

» Distracting loud noise can be reduced by using a range of specific noise-reducing earphones or earplugs, or by listening to music.

» There are a range of strategies that can help to reduce a student's anxiety. Some of these include cognitive behavior therapy, focusing on tasks, reading, and finding a "safe place."

» A travel-training program must always include teaching about stranger danger.

7

Road Crossing

Teaching Road Crossing to the Beginner

Trainers often panic when contemplating how and where to begin teaching the very important skill of road crossing. This is a reasonable response; however, the approaches to teaching road crossing explained in this book have been highly successful. In our communities there are varieties of road crossing types, all of which are trained differently. Commonly, there are:

- **Traffic light crossings:** Some traffic lights have "audio-tactile signals" (ATS) that are specifically designed to assist people with vision and/or hearing impairment to cross the road. The audio-tactile device is a push-button system, which, when pushed, provides pedestrians with audible and tactile signals to indicate when to cross and not to cross the road. One audible signal is a slow pulse which assists pedestrians to locate the push button and indicates that it is not safe to cross. The second signal is a fast pulse which indicates when it is safe to cross the road. The tactile component of the ATS is a vibrating pulse within the push button. A student can rest their hand on the button to feel the pulse. There are two pulses which pulsate in time with the audio signal. The slow pulse indicates it is not safe to cross the road while the fast pulse indicates it is safe to cross the road.

I encourage everyone to use the tactile component of the ATS, not only those with a disability. The main advantage of the ATS is that they keep us safe, especially in high-density traffic environments where two or more ATS crossings are located closely together. How often have you gone to cross the road when you heard an audio signal, only to discover it was the pole on another crossing close by that sounded? Had you also been touching the push button at your crossing you would have realized that the tactile pulse was still slow, indicating it was unsafe to cross the road.

- **Marked crossings:** These include zebra crossings or crosswalks where vehicles are required to stop once a pedestrian is actually on the marked crossing.

- **Unmarked or uncontrolled crossings:** These are road crossing without ATS, traffic signals, or markers of any kind, where vehicles are not required to stop for pedestrians.

There is a general order in which to teach these crossings, from the easiest (where the student is assisted by controls on the crossing) to the more complex (where a student's perception and judgment are required, such as on an uncontrolled crossing). Ideally, only teach one crossing type at a time so that students do not become confused, as each type of crossing has different rules that require different responses from the student. Where practical, the general order to teach road crossings is:

- first, teach crossing at traffic lights (or ATS)

- second, at pedestrian or marked crossings, and

- third, at uncontrolled crossings.

Of course if the student's community only contains one road crossing type, for example, an uncontrolled crossing in a small rural area, then go ahead and teach that crossing.

Crossing the road at traffic lights using audio-tactile signals

Let us assume that the student has never learned to cross a road independently. Teaching a student to cross at an ATS crossing first is helpful because the student learns that there are concrete rules to crossing roads (rather than simply ambling across). The specific rules of crossing at traffic lights are that the student only crosses the road when the green walk light can be seen and/or the quick beep heard and/or the quick tactile feedback is felt under the hand.

Of course, it depends on each student's preferences as to which of these modes the trainer teaches them to focus on. For instance, if the student is tactile defensive (and therefore doesn't want to touch the push button to feel the tactile pulse) they might be taught to look for the green walk light (signifying it is safe to walk) and/or listen to the audio beep. This is completely acceptable and fits well with an individualized training approach.

Always make sure that training is consistent and methodical. That is, once the trainer decides the sequence for teaching a skill, continue teaching the skill in that sequence until the student learns the steps completely. It is less confusing for the student when teaching is methodical and consistent. The following teaching approach has been successfully used with many students.

1. Walk with the student to the traffic light pole. Once at the pole, verbally prompt them to press the button. If a verbal request is not appropriate for that specific student (e.g. they don't respond well to verbal directions) then you might shape their hand to press the button (by placing your hand under theirs and guiding it to the button to push it), or role-model by pressing the button yourself and then shape or guide the student's hand to press the button. Be creative—the goal is for the student to press the button without becoming agitated. Use a calm teaching approach without any stress or tension. Give lots of positive reinforcement *immediately after* the student has

performed the requested action. This usually encourages them to repeat the correct action next time. Give verbal praise if you know the student enjoys this and tell them, "That's terrific, Peter—you have pressed the button."

2. Once the student has pressed the button, encourage them to keep their hand on it so they can feel the tactile pulse. Some students experience tactile defensiveness and will immediately pull back from this (apparently) aversive feeling. That is fine—touching the tactile button is not mandatory but only recommended. But, if the student is happy to touch the button, you might need to hold their hand lightly on it to reinforce the continuity of this action. Some students prefer to put their hand on yours to feel the tactile beeper. Initially, touching your hand might feel safer for the student rather than touching a metal beeper-emitting device. Putting their hand on top of yours also empowers the student in that they have the freedom to take their hand away at any time instead of it being held in position by you.

3. Once the student has pressed the button, stand directly behind them so that you do not block their ability to see clearly to the left and right side of the road. The student should not be able to see you out of the corner of their eye. Standing directly behind your student also gives them a sense of being, to some extent, alone and independent. When the beeper sounds, turn the student's attention to the tactile feeling on their hand. Encourage them to always look right and left for vehicles before walking. Be guided by their natural tendency to direct which side they look first. I recommend that students wait a further three seconds before crossing, to allow straggling vehicles to pass, especially those that drive through a red traffic light. To teach this, you and your student can count to three together, or you can tap your foot three times, or tap your leg with your hand, and then walk. Be inventive—think

of a strategy that is easy for your student to perform to help them to remember to cross after three seconds. If the student will not wait three seconds, having them wear one of the safety colors (see Chapter 6) increases their visibility to drivers.

4. If the student does not initiate walking across the road after three seconds (which they probably won't in the initial stage of training), provide a gentle physical prompt to encourage them to walk (e.g. a gentle hand on the back that lightly moves them forward into a walking motion). *Immediately after* they take that first step onto the road, provide them with positive praise to show they have responded correctly by walking. If the student is a slow walker, then you might encourage them to walk faster by continuing the gentle physical prompt. The purpose of physical prompts and praise is to teach the student the correct way to approach this skill. They are to press the button, wait for the light/ sound/physical pulse, look, wait three seconds, then walk at a reasonable pace across the road.

When teaching, it is essential not to continuously tell the student what to do. In most cases, they will become heavily reliant on these verbal prompts, and the prompts will be difficult to fade. Instead, rely on physical prompts (without talking) and positive reinforcement (only praising the student *after* the student has performed the desired response). Physical prompts and positive reinforcement can be easily and strategically faded out when they are no longer needed.

Crossing the road at a marked/controlled crossing

In Australia, a driver must give way to any pedestrian on or near a pedestrian crossing or marked crossing. This road rule determines the road crossing approach to marked crossings such as pedestrian crossings. The following strategies have been effective for students learning to cross pedestrian crossings.

1. The student's positioning on the crossing, as well as their body language, is important to signal to drivers their intention to cross the road. When drivers are aware that the student wishes to cross the road, they will usually slow down and stop to allow the student to cross. Students need to be positioned safely, but very close to or on the crossing where they are visible to traffic. If the student stands a meter or two (6 feet) away from the crossing and it's unclear whether they wish to cross, or they cannot be seen because of hedges or trees blocking them from a drivers' view, then it's reasonable for drivers not to stop. Once the student is on the edge of the crossing, get them to stand side-on, putting one foot in front of the other, which indicates they are about to walk across the road. This body position signals to drivers very clearly their intention to cross the road. Further, the student can look toward oncoming traffic, which also helps to communicate their desire to cross the road.

2. There are two rules to teach students when crossing at pedestrian crossings. First, if there are no cars, then the student can cross. Second, if there are cars then the cars must have stopped before the student commences crossing the road. If trainers apply these two rules, then most students will learn when it is safe to cross a road.

3. When training your student to cross at marked crossings, stand directly behind them. This is important as you are not blocking their ability to see, and also gives them a sense of being in front and performing the skill more independently. For most of their lives students with disabilities have been told what to do and when to do it. It is time to step back and allow the student opportunities to learn, and to initiate skills and behaviors.

4. If the student does not initiate turning their head to look for cars, then you might like to shape them so that they

learn the correct behavior at a crossing. Observe your student and see which direction they naturally look to first. Whatever their preference—begin in that direction. You might like to tap their right shoulder and point to the right to encourage them to look in that direction. If there are no cars approaching the crossing then you can say, "No cars." Then tap their left shoulder, point to the left, and say, "No cars." You can repeat this process, looking to the right and left again. Once there are no cars, simply give a gentle physical prompt on the back or shoulder that helps the student to begin walking across the road. No talking is required. Once the student takes the first step to cross the road, provide them with plenty of positive reinforcement: "Well done Peter. There are no cars and you are crossing the road." It is always important to say why they have done well, such as "There are no cars," so the student understands exactly what they have performed well and can repeat it next time.

5. If there is a car driving toward the crossing and you have followed the procedure to look both ways, you might point to the car when you see it. Simply say, "Car." Hold the student's attention, perhaps pointing to the oncoming car. Once the car stops at the crossing, point to the car and say, "The car has stopped." Again, provide a gentle physical cue so that the student commences walking. Immediately after they have taken the first step provide positive reinforcement: "Well done Peter. The car has stopped, and you are walking across the road."

6. Repeat these processes until the student begins to initiate taking that first step across the road. Remember, when they initiate the first step without a physical prompt, provide positive reinforcement such as, "That's terrific Peter. The cars have stopped and you are crossing the road." The praise informs Peter that he has performed correctly and this will help to increase his self-confidence.

Crossing the road at an unmarked/ uncontrolled crossing

Sometimes it is difficult to determine the extent of a student's knowledge about the danger of moving vehicles and their ability to cross a road. Often, students with disabilities have been told what to do, and how and when to do it over the course of many years, so it is often difficult to determine what skills students have actually acquired as a result of them observing the environment, and their interaction with it. Now is the chance to see how much they really know about crossing a road.

Before I commence teaching a student how to cross an uncontrolled road, I usually walk with them to the edge of a narrow, quieter road with minimal traffic. I stand behind them and say, "Cross the road when you think it's safe." Of course I am ready to block them from crossing if they make an incorrect decision. If I need to stop the student, I place my hand gently on their shoulder (or wherever is comfortable for them) and point to the car. The only words I say are "That's a car—stop" and point to the car. I avoid negative words like "No. Wrong. Stop walking!" After all, mistakes are part of the learning process and the process needs to be informative and positive.

Asking the student to cross the road when they think it's safe helps me to understand the extent of their understanding about road crossing, vehicle awareness, consequences, and their degree of self-preservation. More often than not, the student cannot quite believe I have asked them to cross the road based on *their* decision. For most of their life they have been told when to cross roads, or been taken through the routine of "look right, look left," then told when to cross anyway. I have stood on the road edge at times for up to 30 minutes while a student internalizes the request to cross. Sometimes a student waits because they believe I will eventually tell them when to cross, or they are trying to apply what they have observed for so many years when being told to cross roads. Students sometimes keep looking for cars, trying to build up the confidence to actually take the first step by themselves and cross the road. When they make a decision and take the first step to cross, you must praise, praise, praise: "Well done Peter. There are no cars and you crossed the road!" Asking the student to cross the road when safe and leaving them to do this breaks a lifelong habit and belief that others will always tell them what to do. Often for the first time, they are drawing on their own capacity as an individual, using their own judgment.

Of course if, after a period of waiting (for example, 10 minutes), it is clear that the student will not cross the road or they consistently make incorrect road crossing decisions, this indicates training is required rather than just building the student's confidence. There might be a number of reasons why they are not initiating road crossing or are making incorrect decisions. For example, they might have been taught to "Stop at the road," and they do—always—and will not go any further without being told to do so; they might genuinely not understand what is involved in this skill or what is expected. Regardless, commence training at a road which has low traffic density, such as a side street where the occasional vehicle drives by. It is important that the student stands where they can clearly see oncoming vehicles and a driver can clearly see the student. You might approach training in the following way:

1. At the edge of the road, stand directly behind the student so that you are out of their line of vision and not blocking their ability to see or hear vehicles. Your positioning will also help the student concentrate on the task at hand, rather than being distracted by you.

2. If needed, assist the student to turn their head to the right-hand side in the direction of oncoming vehicles. (If the student clearly has a preference to turn their head to the left-hand side first, this is fine too.) Point in this direction so that the student can see you. If there are no vehicles, you do not need to say anything. Instead, turn the student's head to the left-hand side and point in that direction. If there are no cars, turn their head to the right side again and point in that direction. If there are no cars, simply say,

"No cars—it's safe," and gently touch the student's back so that they start walking across the road. Notice that you are not actually *telling* the student to cross the road. Instead, you are simply informing them that the conditions are safe to cross. It is of utmost importance after the student takes the very first step to provide encouragement and tell them why they have done so well: "Well done Steve. There are no cars and it's safe to cross the road." This process is laying down the rules for crossing at uncontrolled roads.

3. If a car does approach the crossing during training, stand at the road edge behind your student and help them turn their head in the direction of the car. Point at the car and say, "Car." Exaggerate pointing as the car approaches and is in front of you. Turn the student's head to the other side and repeat this process if a car approaches. Keep turning the student's head until there are no cars, then say, "No cars. It's safe." Gently touch the back of the student so that they commence walking across the road. Provide positive reinforcement immediately after the student has taken the first step: "Well done Steve. There are no cars and it's safe to cross the road."

Over time, and after repeating this training process over weeks or possibly months, the student will most likely begin initiating their first step across the road. The length of time it takes will vary for each student. The student will initiate the first step when they understand the process of crossing the road. They will eventually observe when there are no cars and, because you have provided a lot of praise for taking that first step when there were no cars, will gain enough self-confidence to take the first step across the road. I have worked with parents who have been absolutely amazed at this capacity in their child. They did not believe their child was capable of crossing an uncontrolled road, yet with the opportunity and time to learn, they have done exactly that.

Positioning on the road at uncontrolled crossings

When teaching a student to cross a road you need to consider the safest place for them to cross. The main priority is safety, which must be considered at all times. This means that the student must be highly visible to drivers and they must also be able to see oncoming vehicles very clearly. Here are some tips:

- Avoid crossing at road corners. Crossing at corners is complex as the student is required to look for cars in many directions. Also, if they make an incorrect road crossing decision, cars turning into the corner might not be able to stop without being hit by another vehicle behind them. Instead, teach the student to walk down the road away from the corner to a specific position where they are highly visible to vehicles, and cross the road there.

- When choosing a safe place to cross, make sure the student is not being blocked by trees, foliage, or any other object. Ensure that there is not too much shadow being cast from trees or other items onto the road. The driver's ability to see clearly can be impeded by driving from sunlight into shadow.

- Always avoid crossing at or near roundabouts. Roundabouts are complicated, and drivers are required to concentrate on other cars entering or exiting the roundabout. They have to correctly time their own entry into the roundabout while avoiding colliding with other drivers who do not always know the roundabout rules. Throw a pedestrian into the mix and it's a very precarious situation indeed.

- If a vehicle is parked near an ideal crossing location, have the student walk to the road edge and onto the road next to the front of the parked car so they can be seen by passing vehicles. You might encourage the student to place their hand on the edge of the car to help them stay in that position and not drift in front of or behind the car. This positioning has the benefits of the student being seen by drivers, reducing the distance of the road cross so that the student is on the road for less time, and helping drivers realize that the student intends to cross the road.

When the student can cross quieter uncontrolled roads consistently, safely, and confidently it is time to apply their learning to slightly busier roads. Always remember, however, that if there is a controlled crossing nearby, then it is always safer to use this. Controlled crossings are safer for pedestrians than uncontrolled crossings.

If your student is crossing successfully at an uncontrolled road where there are frequent vehicles passing, then they might have to wait quite a long while until there are "no cars" and it is safe to cross. In these situations, you can teach your student to use a distant landmark as a "marker." This marker will serve as an indicator about whether the student has enough time to cross the road safely. The marker might be a brightly colored house in the distance or a particularly large tree which does not appear anywhere else in that location. You can teach your student the rule that once a car has passed the marker toward them then it is no longer safe to cross the road. Conversely, if the car has not yet reached the marker, they have time to cross the road safely. The trainer must use their judgment wisely and pick a marker that the student can see clearly, ensure that the student is able to apply this method consistently, and ensure that the marker is far enough away to allow time for the student to safely cross the road.

KEY POINTS

» There is a general order in which to teach road crossing: first, at traffic lights, second, at pedestrian crossings, and third, at uncontrolled crossings.

» The student's positioning and body language convey their intention to cross the road to drivers.

» When crossing at pedestrian crossings, ensure that the student is clearly visible to drivers.

» When crossing uncontrolled roads, ensure that the student crosses away from the corner of the road and is clearly visible to drivers.

» Avoid crossing roads at roundabouts.

» When crossing roads, the student must carry a bag or wear an item of clothing from the waist up in bright red, bright yellow, or bright orange (the safety colors) to increase their visibility and safety. Get them to think, "Where's my red hat?" before they head out the door.

8

Other Very Important Travel-Training Skills

Money handling

Some students with a disability understand that they need to exchange coins or paper money to receive an item, but beyond that their comprehension is limited. This does not matter. They only need to have the skill of exchanging money for an item they want to buy—that's all. Rather than have your student depend on someone else to buy things for them, you can teach them to simply hand over money to the cashier (e.g. $10.00), then turn their hand over and, with their arm extended, wait for their change. Because handing over money and waiting for change are such everyday events, most cashiers assume their customers know exactly what they are doing and expect to receive change. This simple method of "bluff" will usually ensure that your student will receive change even though they might not know exactly how much change they are supposed to receive. The point is that they will be highly likely to receive their change. A hint—make sure your student is equipped with a $5 or $10 note, rather than expecting them to manipulate change.

Communication skills

When teaching students to travel in the community, it is important they are able to initiate communication and be understood by others. There are many communication options and methods available to assist people with a disability in communicating, even if their speech is limited or hard for others to understand. A simple and cheap yet effective method is a cue card: a small durable card usually kept in the student's wallet with information or a request written on it. This cue card is handed to a person who reads it and provides a response. The student can hand their cue card (say) to a railway attendant or a bus driver to communicate, "May I have a pensioner ticket please?" or a cue card handed to a shop assistant or bus driver might say, "I'm lost, can you please phone my dad John on [a specific telephone number…]," or a cue card handed to a cashier might say, "Can I have a hamburger with chips, please?" Some people who rely on several cue cards with various messages carry a cue card holder so they can flip through the cards quickly to find the one they are looking for to use in a particular situation.

Some people use augmentative and alternative communication (AAC) devices, or devices such as iPads or mobile phones with applications that have voice output. The devices are easy to set up and use, and can generate a voice request when a button or two are touched.

Recently, I was in a take-away food outlet and observed a young man with Down syndrome who had limited speech order his lunch using his mobile phone. When he pressed a button on the phone, it emitted the request "Can I have a hamburger, small fries, and a small orange juice please?" The cashier understood the request easily, and was clearly impressed with this device and the young man's ability to use it.

Phone skills

Mobile phone

It is useful for a student to carry a mobile phone when traveling. The student can be taught to phone a specific person to confirm their arrival at a destination. Importantly, others can contact them if they have not arrived at their destination, or are late arriving. A student might not be able to speak into the phone, but they might be able to send a text message, or answer the phone to hear a message. Alternatively, students can be taught to give the phone with a cue card to a "safe person" (for example, "a mother with a pram" or a cashier) with the card requesting they ring [the name of a significant other] if the student needs to talk to that person or send them a message. Often, mobile phones can be preprogrammed so that the user only has to press a button or two to ring a specific person. There are also many adapted mobile phones that are easier to use (such as phones with larger-sized buttons that text-message in symbols rather than words).

Parents often worry that their child will probably lose the phone. Ideas that have been successful in preventing this include:

- Wearing the phone in a neat small pocket or pouch around the neck.

- Sewing a pocket on the inside of a shirt or school jumper, which adds to the security of the phone.

- Attaching the phone to the inside of the student's school backpack using a retractable cord inside the bag. When the phone is being used, it remains on the cord, and when not in use it remains in the bag on the cord.

- Installing software on the phone that allows parents to track and locate the phone. This software only works if the phone battery is charged so keeping the phone charged is a very important skill to teach a student. Often, when introducing the mobile to a student you also teach them the habit of charging the phone every night (or at a time of day that suits the student).

Public phones

Public phone boxes are becoming a rare sight on today's streets, but those that still exist tend to be located near shops, public transport areas, or shopping centers. Sometimes, it is useful to teach a student how to use a public phone even if they carry a mobile phone. A public phone can be a back-up strategy when the mobile is broken, lost, or not charged. The student can keep a phone card or some coins in their wallet specifically for using in public phones. I remember working with a young girl with a learning impairment who had the great idea of wrapping her "phone coins" in aluminum foil and keeping them in her wallet, just in case she ever needed to make a phone call. The aluminum foil helped her remember that these coins were specifically for the public phone rather than for spending at the school canteen.

Sometimes students find it difficult to remember a phone number. If this is the case then they can keep a cue card in their wallet so they have the number in front of them when dialing. If the student can't use a cue card, then they can carry a piece of cardboard with holes cut out, corresponding to the numbers they need to dial on a push-button phone. Through repetition, a student can be taught to press these numbers in a particular order. Some students have found that coloring around the cut-out squares in different colors helps them to memorize the number order. Remember to incorporate whatever method helps the student in their training.

Time awareness

When traveling, it is important that the student has some awareness of time. It might be that the student needs to know the time their bus arrives, if they have missed the train or bus, the time to arrive at work, or the time to leave an activity. Usually people look at their watches or mobile devices to tell the time, but many people with a disability find it hard to learn the concept of time or to use watches or clocks. In such cases, two strategies can be used to assist students.

First, alarms can be used. A wristwatch or mobile phone with an alarm can be set to go off when the student needs to leave work or any other activity. Or an alarm can be set to remind the student when they should be on the bus or train. If the alarm sounds and they are not on the bus or train, the transport might be late. In such cases, the student might be taught that if the alarm sounds and they are not on the bus, they should telephone a parent or teacher informing them they have missed the bus.

Sometimes students walk slowly and run the risk of being late for work. An alarm can remind the student to speed up if they have not arrived at their destination. Some students require two or more alarms to alert them along a route. For example, a young man with Asperger syndrome enjoyed watching trains coming into his local train station. Once he arrived at the station, he was given ten minutes to watch the trains. At ten minutes, his wristwatch alarm sounded, which reminded him he needed to start walking to the bus stop. He was a slow walker. After he exited his bus to walk to work, a second alarm from a small alarm clock sounded in his bag. This alarm reminded him he had to walk faster so that he would reach work in time.

A second strategy is using tracking devices and "reminder apps" that use global positioning system (GPS) locators. Tracking devices can be built into a shoe, wristwatch, or tag, and are available in a variety of forms. An internet search will reveal the types of tracking devices that are available. GPS tracking devices send the observer (e.g. parents) an email or text message to alert them of the student's location. Since the observer can see the location of the student, if they are late, then the observer can call the student on their mobile to provide a verbal prompt to "hurry up" so they arrive at their destination on time. There are also "reminder apps" for mobile phones that can be set to tell the student when to "Walk to the bus stop" or to "Leave the room and go to lunch."

Bus travel

When a student is ready to learn how to use public transport and there are both trains and buses available, I prefer to teach buses first. Buses are mostly controlled environments with fewer people traveling at one time, and the driver is close by if needed by the student. There are about eight steps to teaching bus travel, but with consistent and positive training your student will succeed. Before commencing bus training, plan the steps ahead of time rather than when you are training your student. When you are with your student, just focus on the important task of teaching.

Step 1: Where to stand at the bus stop

Once the student arrives at the bus stop it is important that they stand where the driver can see them and where they can see the bus. Teach your student to stand at the bus stop, if possible, rather than sitting, as I have found students can easily get distracted and miss their bus. Look for a landmark that the student will remember, marking the place where they will stand. Landmarks can be, for example, the actual bus pole if it is not too close to the road or a marker on the ground such as a drain cover, a wide crack, or a discolored pavement tile. Just ensure that the landmark is permanent and it will be there the next time both of you are at the bus stop. When the student has positioned themselves on or near the landmark, have them take their pass or cash out of their bag so that they are prepared to enter the bus efficiently.

Step 2: Identifying the correct bus

Some students find identifying their bus difficult because they do not remember their bus number. If this is the case, identify only one bus for your student to catch (even though there might be several buses that go to the destination). Write the bus number on a cue card and when your student arrives at the bus stop, have them take out the cue card so they can refer to it as each bus comes by. Many students are able to match the cue card with the bus number with a little bit of training. However, if your student finds this difficult they can also practice matching at home. You might make a large sign with the bus number printed on it and stick this in a prominent place, for example, on their bedroom wall. Once every two days or so when the student's in a receptive mood you might have them take the cue card from their wallet and practice matching the bus number to the number on the wall. Even when they are not practicing matching they can still observe the bus number on the wall, which will help them memorize it.

In rarer instances, students might not be able to match their bus number using a cue card with the number on the bus. Instead, they have successfully held up large cards with the bus number written down in large black print for the bus driver to read as they slow down. Most drivers, when they see the number, will stop for the student. Other students have boarded the bus and asked the driver, perhaps even using a cue card, if this was the "bus to Brighton" or "the 423 bus."

GPS technology can also be used, if needed, to assist the student. There are apps that tell the student that their bus is approaching the bus stop. If you have a travel-related problem, there is probably an app or other piece of technology that can solve it. We only have to search for these. Be creative and use your student's strengths to figure out a way for that student to board their correct bus.

Step 3: Hailing the bus

Once the student has identified the correct bus, they must learn to hail or stop the bus. In most situations, if a student waves an extended arm above their head toward the bus, then the driver will stop to let them board. Teach your student to always hail a bus this way, even if their bus routinely pulls into the stop. They might need to actively hail a bus in a different situation later on, so this is an important skill for them to learn.

Step 4: Paying the fare

There are several methods to pay a bus fare. In most countries students can purchase a bus travel card that is either inserted into, or tapped onto, a machine just inside the bus. Some students also have bus passes to show the driver as they enter the bus. Less frequently, passengers pay with coins. Paying a bus fare with coins is best avoided, if possible, as this can bring unnecessary complication to the process of boarding a bus and paying the correct fare.

When entering the bus, it can be useful for the student to give the driver a written note requesting they stop at a particular bus stop, for example, "Can you stop at Chambers Street and tell me it's my bus stop, please." For this purpose you can use post-it-notes —small pieces of sticky-backed paper—that the driver can stick in the middle of the steering wheel to help them remember the request. Presenting the driver with the request note is a good back-up strategy in case the student forgets to ring the bus bell to exit the bus.

Step 5: Where to sit on the bus

If possible, teach your student to sit close to the bus driver toward the front of the bus. From this position, they can exit the bus more easily than if they had to walk through a crowded bus to get to the exit door; they are also close to the driver if they need assistance, or if the driver needs to tell them they have arrived at their stop and now need to get off the bus. Also teach your student how to stand safely on a moving bus in case there are no seats available.

Step 6: Ringing the bell to exit the bus

The trainer and student need to decide which environmental landmark the student will use as a cue to ring the bell to exit the bus. The landmark needs to be relevant and prominent to the student, and far enough away from the right bus stop to give the driver time to stop. Some landmarks that students have used have been brightly colored fast-food symbols near the roadside, particular petrol station logos, or a prominent colored building that is familiar to the student.

If the student isn't familiar with a prominent landmark, such as a petrol station, you might need to familiarize them with it to make it more important in their life. One student's mother identified a bright orange petrol station as an excellent landmark for her son. Because this landmark was unfamiliar to him, she drove there numerous times with him to buy petrol, and also allowed him to buy a favorite treat. This station became very important and positive to the son, which made it easy for him to remember the landmark when traveling in the bus. It was then quite easy for the mother to teach her son to ring the bus bell when he saw this favored petrol station.

There are also GPS technologies that can assist a student, such as apps that tell them when they are approaching their bus stop. They can also use the app to see the location of their bus and their bus stop if they want to track the bus route. This can be a great method to maintain the student's concentration if they enjoy technology rather than risking them daydreaming or falling asleep.

Step 7: Teaching a back-up strategy

So you think that training is going well and the student is beginning to initiate ringing the bus bell and exiting the bus. The student's confidence has also increased and they are feeling good about traveling on the bus. If this is the case, then it's probably a good time to introduce a back-up strategy just in case one day the bus drives past the bus stop when the student is traveling alone. These situations do happen and we always need to train for the "what-ifs."

Teach the student that if the driver passes their stop, then they need to ring the bus bell immediately so that they can get off at the next bus stop. If the next stop is too dangerous (if there is no safe road crossing area) then the student can approach the bus driver to seek help. I have observed an occasion where the student asked for help and the driver stopped the bus. The student gave the driver her mobile phone, asking him to ring her mother. The driver rang the mother and explained what had happened, and told her where her daughter was so she could come and collect her. Think of the best alternatives if the driver does drive past the student's stop, and teach what to do in this case.

Trainers can teach this back-up strategy by driving the bus route with the student and going to look at the next bus stop. From this bus stop you might teach the student the walking route back to their correct exit stop. Then, once again, travel on the bus past the usual bus stop and let the student ring the bell and get off at the next one. Observe the student walk back to the correct exit bus stop. Repeat this procedure to ensure that they are confident and know what to do in this situation.

Step 8: Fading out from training

The process of fading out from teaching has been described in Chapter 5. When training on the bus, you initially need to sit close to the student. You might sit next to them to teach them to ring the bus bell, and provide positive reinforcement (praise) when they see the landmark and ring the bell. After a number of training sessions, you might notice that they see the landmark petrol station and ring the bell without any prompting from you. If this occurs over a few training sessions, then you might conclude that the student has learned this skill.

Now is the time to start fading yourself out of the training situation so the student can reliably perform this step without you being beside them. For example, you might start sitting two seats away from them next time you travel on the bus together, and set a performance criterion for five training sessions. That is, with you sitting two seats away and *providing no prompting and no reinforcement* the student needs to ring the bus bell over five consecutive sessions and initiate getting off at the right stop. If they do this successfully they have met the criterion you set, so you might then sit a further four to five seats away from them, and set another criterion of five times.

Of course, if the student forgets to ring the bell on any occasion, then you move closer to prompt and/or reinforce the behavior before fading out again. If the student repeats the correct behavior successfully five consecutive times, then you gradually move back further into the bus. You would repeat this pattern of setting the criterion and observing until you were near the back of the bus. This entire process might take 25 weeks or more, which feels like a long time, but after this period you can confidently know that your student is safe. The benefit is that you would have observed them 25 times on the bus under varying circumstances and conditions such as different weather (sun, rain, snow), possibly dealing with other people in the bus, perhaps dealing with a moody bus driver, or a driver who drove past the student's stop. If the student responds safely and correctly in all these situations, then you can be confident they are "travel safe" on this route.

Train travel

Train travel is usually taught later, when the student is a fairly confident traveler and has traveled at least two walking routes independently. Train travel is more complex because of the large number of people traveling at one time where many more random events can occur (e.g. angry passengers, crying babies, boisterous school children, and train breakdowns). Also, the student needs to decipher more information about train destinations, platform numbers, and train cancellations, which can be overwhelming for an unconfident traveler. Like bus travel, there are structured steps to teaching this skill, and even greater consideration must be given to back-up strategies to prepare students for inevitable random events. Phone skills and communication skills are vital when traveling on trains and these must be taught as part of the travel-training program before the student is declared independent on a particular route.

There are six basic steps to teaching train travel which need to be planned before training your student.

Step 1: Purchasing the train ticket

There are several ways to purchase train tickets, depending on where your student lives. Identify the most user-friendly way for your student, such as a "tap on/tap off" card. This system is simple for students to learn, especially if a parent takes care of loading the card with credit and managing the card's balance.

As a back-up strategy in case the card is lost or there is no money left on the card, also teach the student to purchase a ticket from the railway attendant.

Step 2: Identifying the correct train platform

Once the student has purchased their ticket and entered the train station, proceed to the destination board which lists destinations, interim stops, and platform numbers. For example, on Platform 1 the next train destination might be Stanmore, and the train stops at Central, Redfern, Macdonaldtown, Newtown, and Stanmore. It is important that the student learns to check the destination board every trip, as their train might not always leave from the same train platform. Changes regularly occur, particularly at major stations where many trains arrive and depart at the same time.

Once at the destination board the student can take out a cue card (if needed) to help match and locate the destination. For example, if their destination is Newtown, have this written on a cue card, and teach the student to search each board methodically from top to bottom and from left to right to locate Newtown. Once they locate Newtown, teach them to then look at the train platform number this train leaves from, and to proceed to that platform.

Step 3: Where to stand and wait for the train

Safety must always be considered when traveling on public transport. Sitting in the carriage next to the driver's carriage is highly recommended so that, if needed, the student can attract the attention of the driver or guard. Have the student stand on the platform near where the driver's carriage will stop. Choose a landmark for them to stand near, or teach them to always get in the door two back from the front of the train.

Some years ago a mother taught her daughter train travel so that she could commute to and from work. The student was taught to travel in the carriage next to the driver's carriage. One afternoon, a group of young boys boarded her carriage, took her bag, and ran through the train with it. Of course the student was distraught and, as she had been taught, knocked loudly and continuously on the driver's door. An attendant opened the door and the student explained what had happened. After a short search for the boys, her bag was retrieved and she emerged confident from this experience.

Most train carriages in large cities have an emergency button. When it is pushed, the train will come to a stop and the train guard will investigate why the button was pushed. If you believe your student will only press this button in a real emergency (illness or harassment), then it is also worth incorporating pushing this button into the training program. Sometimes you can organize with the train company to teach your student on a carriage that is not in use. This is an appropriate time to teach them to press the emergency button without negative consequences.

Step 4: Getting ready to exit the train

Knowing which station to exit the train is essential. There are a few strategies to accomplish this, depending on the skills of your student. A useful tip for most students is to identify a landmark that will prompt the student that theirs is the next stop. This landmark might be a railway tunnel, a particularly unusual building, or even the name of the preceding station. Once the student sights this landmark, they are to begin preparing to exit the train and walk toward the exit door.

Some students have successfully used a "flip cue card book" that contains cards, each with the name of one station. It does not matter if the student can read each card or match it to the station as they will still know that the last card means they must get off the train. For example, as the train passes Redfern station, the student flips the Redfern card over to reveal the Macdonaldtown card, which is the next station. As they pass Macdonaldtown station they flip over again to reveal Newtown station, which is their destination. This is the final card in the flip book and an indicator to exit the train. Once the final card has been reached, it is time to move to the exit door. Although there might be an audio system in the train informing passengers of the next stop, sometimes this system does not work or is difficult to understand. It is important to teach the other methods mentioned in case the audio is out of order or inaudible.

Step 5: Teaching back-up strategies

Teaching back-up strategies when traveling on public transport is essential because inevitably something will go wrong. I have observed train drivers forgetting to stop at particular stations; trains breaking down and stopping in "no man's land" with confused passengers waiting for up to an hour or so; and trains arriving very late at their destination. Whatever occurs, your student needs to be equipped with skills and knowledge to cope in these situations.

Once you believe that your student is traveling confidently on the train and is demonstrating the relevant skills, it is time to introduce back-up strategies. Teach back-up strategies *before* you commence fading out from the program because you need to be in close contact with the student to teach the required skills. Fading out means that you are distancing yourself from the student once they start to demonstrate they can perform steps independently— so you do not want to return to their side to teach back-up strategies. This can be demoralizing for the student who has started to believe that they do not need you anymore.

The main back-up skills involve you teaching the student about the one or two train stops after their stop, including the next major stop on that train line, in case they miss their stop, and requesting assistance, or seeking assistance using a phone or cue card. Let's look at each of these in turn.

First, teach your student about the next one or two train stops after their station, including the next major train stop. Explain that sometimes the train might forget to stop at their station, in which case they must get off at the next stop. The next stop is generally the next station or, on some express passenger services, the next major station from which many trains depart, and where large numbers of people can be traveling to a range of destinations. To teach this back-up strategy, travel through the student's stop on the train, and then get off at the next stop with them. Familiarize them to the destination board and how to read it so they can take a train back to their original destination, or teach the location of the train attendants in case they need to ask for help. Second, teach your student to ring their significant person (family member/teacher/friend) on either their mobile phone or a public phone to let them know about their current situation. If the student is unable to use a phone, then ensure they can use a cue card to seek assistance. They might approach a train attendant and give them the cue card that requests help to return to their original desired destination or to make a phone call to their significant person. Most importantly, the student needs to feel comfortable about what to do, even if the train goes past their destination. Teach these skills as part of travel-training, and have the student demonstrate their knowledge of what to do in the situation a number of times. Once you have observed the student successfully demonstrate this knowledge many times independently, then you can continue to fade out from training.

Step 6: Fading out from training

Once you have observed the student demonstrating independent train travel skills, such as locating the correct train platform, waiting for the train at the correct place, boarding safely, identifying the correct place to prepare to exit the train, exiting successfully, and demonstrating back-up strategies, you are ready to commence fading out your presence from this program.

Initially, you might stand about 2 to 3 meters (9 feet) from your student on the platform while they wait for their train. Once on the train, sit three to four seats away from them, preferably behind them so they cannot directly see you. You might set a performance criterion of observing from this position three times over three consecutive training sessions. Once the student has accomplished this three times, you might move further back on the platform and in the train, to about six to seven seats away. Again set the criterion: perhaps another three times. Once this has been accomplished you might move to the very back of the carriage and set another criterion of three to four times. Once achieved, you can move into another carriage so that the student cannot see you (although ensure that you can still see them). You might set a higher success criterion of eight to ten observations at this point, because the student and public will think the student is alone and it allows time to observe various situations that can occur.

Some common situations I have observed are students engaging in natural behaviors (e.g. twirling their hair or talking softly to themselves) rather than behaving the way they did when the trainer was with them. Only rarely have I seen students suddenly misbehaving or acting inappropriately at this point in their program. Instead, they are usually feeling so pleased with themselves and their accomplishment that these feelings promote appropriate behavior. Sometimes I have observed a traveler next to the student request the time or start a conversation. During the training program the student is taught to act appropriately and can often handle these situations. However, if an incident does occur I recommend you observe it and the student's reaction to it. Depending on the situation (and if it is not life threatening), I suggest you wait to see if the student can problem solve. You do not want to prematurely interfere but rather assess the student's coping skills. I remember one incident when a train broke down. I waited to see my student's reaction. During the program he had been taught that if anything happened that distressed him, he was to phone his mother or knock on the train guard's door to ask for help. It took about five minutes for the student to realize something out of the ordinary had happened. He observed the other passengers and kept looking out of the window. After about

15 minutes, when the other passengers became frustrated and confused because they had not been told why the train had stopped, he rang his mother. She advised him to sit there patiently and she would find out what had happened and call him back. She then rang the railway who informed her of the problem. She rang her son back, told him they were fixing the problem and that he had done so well to ring her and to just keep sitting in his seat until the train started again. She also asked him to call her when the train started (so that she could praise his efforts). Needless to say I was thrilled at his handling of this situation and he came away from the experience with even more self-confidence.

However, if the student had not called his mother and was clearly distressed I would have intervened and trained him to deal with this situation. I would have coached him through deciding the best action to take, and reinforced him taking the correct action, such as ringing his mother. Sometimes teaching in real-life situations offers the student learning opportunities with lessons they always remember.

KEY POINTS

» Waiting for change with an open hand and arm extended is an important money-handling skill.

» Being able to initiate communication and being understood by others is an essential skill that can be achieved in a variety of ways.

» Using mobile phones and public phones are important aspects of travel-training programs.

» There are many strategies to assist your student to become aware of the time regardless of whether or not they are able to tell the time or understand the concept of time.

» Bus travel is usually taught before train travel.

» Always teach back-up strategies before fading out.

9

Travel-Training in Schools with Student Groups with Disabilities

It is never too early to start travel-training. I have started travel-training with parents and their young babies with a variety of disabilities. These babies eventually grew into teenagers with excellent independent travel skills, able to confidently and safely negotiate public transport, road crossing, and safety strategies without difficulty.

When young people with a disability start school, school provides an ideal environment to continue the development of travel-training skills. Students often spend much of their time with the same teachers who can provide frequent and consistent training. Ideally, travel-training can continue from infancy through to preschool then primary school and into high school, with students learning skills to handle progressively more complex routes and situations.

Teachers typically teach groups of children and have a very important role when it comes to travel-training. The emphasis of travel-training at school is not so much on students learning to travel independently (which will happen later or concurrently— often out of hours— with more intensive one-to-one training) but rather on learning vital travel-related skills and behaviors that lay the foundation for independent travel.

Preparation for travel-training

There is a typical order of teaching travel-training skills in the school setting, commencing from very simple to complex skills. Each skill is equally important and builds upon the one learned previously. Some examples follow.

Where's my red hat/shirt *or* bright orange scarf *or* bright yellow bag?

As mentioned previously, I recommend that students wear one of these safety colors from the waist up to increase their visibility, and therefore safety, when traveling. The goal is for students to automatically reach for their red hat before they walk out the door. This is important because ideally, you would like that young student to wear a brightly colored item when they are traveling in their communities when they are 20, 30, 40, 50+ years of age, so they will always be as safe as possible.

I think back over the years to the clever ways that teachers have trained their students to put on their red hats (or other brightly colored items) before walking out their classroom door. I recall teachers walking with small groups of primary school students to the local shop to choose their own red hat or scarf, making the outing a fun adventure for the students. After the students had chosen their hats or scarves, they walked back to school wearing them, with the teachers remarking how wonderful they all were, how great they all looked, and how drivers could now see them clearly when crossing roads. This was the beginning of the teachers emphasizing the importance of wearing a safety-colored item of clothing to the students. When they returned to the classroom, the teachers spent time helping them decide where they would keep their brightly colored items so that they knew where to find them next time they went out. The teachers had installed colorful hooks on the walls and cupboards within the students' reach, as well as exciting nooks and crannies that looked like magic caves and secret hideaways. After each student had chosen their special place, the student and teacher painted their name or special symbol near their item to help them remember its location. From that day, whenever the students went on their travel-training adventures, they went to their hook or special place and put on their "red hat" before walking out the door. Eventually this student behavior became automatic and teachers did not need to prompt the students to put their item on. This "where's my red hat?" strategy was also replicated in the students' homes with great success.

Building self-confidence

At school there are lots of opportunities to help students build their self-confidence in readiness for travel-training. Self-confidence is a prerequisite to independent travel and equips the student with the motivation to learn and cope in different travel situations.

To increase their confidence, teachers give younger students opportunities to choose "special traveling tasks" within the school. This has included walking to the school canteen to place their classes' lunch orders, walking to the office to request items from the office staff, returning a book that was used in class by the teacher to the library, or taking an "important note" from their teacher to the principal. These tasks, shared among students, provide them with opportunities such as choosing which task they would like to do; walking independently on a route; feeling important and relevant; using social etiquette such as please and thank you, and waiting for an older person to walk through the door first; and learning to share pathways. All of these skills contribute to trouble-free travel.

Purchasing items at the school canteen

It is also important to provide students with opportunities to purchase items at the school canteen. Skills learned at the canteen can be generalized to making purchases in supermarkets or other shops in the community.

The skills students learn at the canteen include money preparation (taking money out of their wallet ready to make the purchase); choosing the item that they would like to buy; learning the etiquette around queuing behind people at an appropriate distance and waiting patiently until it is their turn; giving money to the cashier; and, importantly, keeping their hand out while waiting for their change. Don't worry if the student does not understand the value of money or cannot add the change. The most important point of keeping their hand out is the "bluff"—the cashier *thinks* they know they must receive change and the student is more often than not assured of receiving the correct change. I have worked with many young adults who did not have the benefit of making purchases earlier in their lives or at school. The typical consequences of this lack of experience have been that they are unsure of how to get money out of their wallet; they are unsure about how to choose items or understand the number of items they can buy; they rush to the counter to buy their item ahead of others instead of queuing and waiting their turn; they stand too close or too far from others in a queue, or do not understand they must queue if others are also waiting to be served; they lose concentration and start daydreaming, which frustrates the cashier and customers around them; they walk away after making a purchase without taking their change; or they simply lack the confidence to make purchases in shops. These aspects are much easier to teach if we introduce students to the skills of purchasing items at a young age.

Walking the block

Teachers often introduce travel-training to a small group of students, usually up to six at a time. With younger students, an appropriate way to introduce travel-training outside the school grounds is to walk a block route that does not include road crossing. Road crossing is complicated and can be left for a later time once the student has acquired a little more emotional maturity and confidence. A block route, however, still exposes students to driveways and pathways—two aspects that require a specific set of responses.

First, it is important for students to learn that pedestrians must share the pathways with each other. If we are in Australia, then pedestrians walk on the left-hand side of the path. Eventually, when the student is older and walking in much busier environments, being able to apply this simple rule will make travel a lot easier.

Second, students need to become aware of driveways and that vehicles can enter and exit them. Teachers need to introduce the concept of stopping at a driveway and looking for vehicles entering or exiting the driveway. Importantly, if a vehicle is present the student must learn to stop. An important teaching tip here is that if the car stops on a driveway to allow a student to cross, then teach the student to "wave the car on." This will make it clear to the driver that the pedestrian is in control and will wait until the car has driven away. This is likely to prevent driver/pedestrian confusion and keep both the pedestrian and driver safe. However, when there are no cars, the student can walk across the driveway and continue on their way. If the student learns to look, identify whether or not a vehicle is present, and responds to that appropriately, then they are ready to take on more complex routes.

Please note that the more able a student becomes on crossing driveways, the less likely they will come to a complete stop as they did when they were learning this skill. This is okay. If we notice our own behavior, we often observe a driveway a meter or two before we have reached it and when we arrive at it we have already assessed whether or not it is safe to cross. We rarely come to a complete stop. If we want students to progress as travelers and they have shown that they have learned skills which they apply successfully and consistently, we must let them adapt their behavior to suit their own personality and level of confidence. Remember, they are also wearing their red hat, increasing their visibility to vehicles.

Crossing at traffic lights

Once students are fairly competent at walking block routes, trainers can move on to routes with traffic light crossings. Teaching this type of crossing is discussed in Chapter 7. It is challenging to teach a group of six students how to cross at this crossing type. Each student will have varying skills and understanding of crossing at traffic lights, and it is logistically difficult to have every student press the button on the traffic light pole. Instead, have some fun and appoint a "leader" for each task. I have observed that students respond positively to the teacher's "designated leader" in a couple of ways. First, because the designated student is receiving positive attention from the teacher, the other students observe more closely what the lead student does to get that level of attention, such as pressing the traffic light button and standing calmly and quietly waiting for the correct time to cross the road. Second, it encourages other students to want to become the leader. The consequence of being the leader of an activity is that the student receives a small amount of focused training, a lot of praise and positive attention, and they feel important, which assists in increasing their self-confidence. There are good feelings associated with being a leader, regardless of the personality of the student. Students also tend to observe each other and learn from each other a little more than the teacher, who they have to attend to most of the time.

Even developing a student's confidence to walk ahead of the teacher or student group can be encouraged by using a "you-are-the-leader" strategy. Again, training must be fun and encouraging. Start the game, if you can, with a confident student who will be a good role model, exhibiting what to do and how to do it so that the other students can observe the correct behavior. You might say, "Okay. Now Suzie is going to lead the group! Off you go Suzie—out to the front of the group!" Suzie will walk ahead of the group on the correct side of the path with the other students and teachers following. This is a training opportunity, so teachers will remark aloud about how good Suzie is walking on the left side of the path; what a good speed she's walking at; how wonderful her "red hat" looks; how well she looks for cars at the driveway (possibly waving some idling cars on); and when there are no cars, "What a terrific crossing she has made." Suzie will feel so fantastic and these vital lessons are being reinforced not only to Suzie but to the other students in the group. Then it might be Steve's turn. "Great leading, Suzie. Okay Steve, now it's your turn. Terrific—you are the leader of the group…" The less confident students will need encouragement and shaping to take the lead. That is fine—just have fun and help your students succeed at this task. The point of this exercise is that to become an independent traveler, students need to have the confidence to start walking ahead of the trainer.

Crossing at pedestrian crossings

Once you believe the students have a basic understanding about the process of crossing at traffic lights you can move on to more complex controlled road crossings like pedestrian crossings. At school, students do not need to be able to cross roads totally independently. The one-to-one training to enable them to develop the confidence to cross independently can be done outside of school hours. The process of training students to cross at pedestrian crossings is discussed in Chapter 7. However, teachers can replicate the "designated leader game" to role-model how to cross at pedestrian crossings. As always, have fun and be encouraging. We want all students to equate travel-training with positive feelings.

Crossing at uncontrolled crossings

As discussed in Chapter 7, learning to cross at uncontrolled crossings is the last road crossing skill to teach students because of its complexity. Role-modeling by teachers and highly competent students is very important, allowing other students to observe and learn. For example, the teacher might point out to the group the landmark where they will cross the road (e.g. at the bright green mailbox). Everyone in the group might move close to the mailbox and discuss its features (such as its color, what it sounds like when you tap against it, its shape, and height) to help students remember the landmark and what a landmark is (i.e. a unique object in the environment that is permanent, and serves as a marker or a reminder that this is the safe point to cross the road). The teacher or highly competent student will repeat the road crossing process discussed in Chapter 7. Often, two teachers accompany a small group of students. After the first teacher has role-modeled the way to cross the road, followed by a highly competent student, the other students can also have a go. One teacher can shape each student to cross the road while the first teacher waits on the other side to receive the students with lots of praise, and to be with the students who have already crossed.

Options, choice, and planning

Another important aspect of travel-training at school is learning about options, choice, and planning. For example, at the beginning of the week the teacher can ask the students, "What day will we walk to the shop to buy something?" Would they like to go shopping on Tuesday or Thursday? Also, which route would they like to take? Would they like to take the pedestrian crossing route or the traffic lights route? What would they like to buy—a sandwich or a drink? You might also like to introduce the concept of voting on an outcome, for example, "Hands up if you'd like to go on Tuesday? Hands up if you'd like to go on Thursday? Right—two students want to go on Tuesday though four students want to go on Thursday. Because more students want to go on Thursday, we will go on Thursday." Be creative and introduce two options—more if the students will succeed in choosing which option they might like. Importantly, this and every exercise must be achievable and fun so that students have the maximum opportunity to learn.

Mobile phone and public phone use

Ideally, introduce one or both of these communication methods into school-based travel-training. Using a phone to make a call independently or with assistance is an essential life skill for students, especially if the expectation is that they will ultimately travel independently. Upon reaching a destination, it is a good idea for the student to call a significant other to confirm their arrival. This back-up strategy ensures the person's safety, and should be included in every travel-training program.

An effective way to introduce phone use into the travel-training program is, before leaving the classroom, to discuss the importance of phoning a friend/parent when they arrive at the shop. After the discussion, present the mobile phone to a student who places it safely in their bag. Once the students have arrived at the shop, choose a quiet location outside and the student who carried the phone can be shown how to make the call. Gather the other students around because this is an excellent training opportunity. The student making the call might phone the school secretary or their mother (who will be waiting for the call). Have the phone number written on a cue card so that all the students can see it. You might assist the student to dial each number. When the call is answered ask the student to tell the school secretary (or mother) that, "We are at the shop," and when the conversation has finished, show the students how to hang up. If this process is followed on all travel-training routes, then students will learn that ringing another person when they arrive at a destination is very important, and an integral part of traveling somewhere.

Making a purchase

When students start travel-training outside of school hours, walking to the local shop and purchasing an item is often one of the first travel-training goals. It is, therefore, important for students to learn how to purchase an item when learning prerequisite travel-training skills at school. Many schools include cooking classes and, as part of this subject, students may purchase the items needed for their recipe. This provides a purposeful travel-training outing to the supermarket that incorporates many learning opportunities for students. For example, students can be given a list of two to three items each. When they arrive at the supermarket they can be assisted to locate their items (where they learn about similar items being grouped together, and how to read the location of items), choose which of the similar items they want (based on package size or price), put the items in their shopping basket, take them to the counter where they might be required to queue, place the items on the conveyer belt when it's their turn, pay for the items, wait for change, then exit the shop. Another benefit of shopping is that each student experiences being responsible for their own groceries. They learn to pack the groceries into their bag and return to school and use them in their cooking class. Of course they eventually get to eat their cooking which makes the entire process of walking to the shop, buying items, and returning to school meaningful.

Introducing public transport

Using public transport is complicated because it involves dealing with the public and students require a level of self-confidence. Ideally, introduce students to bus and train travel after they have participated in the travel-training activities discussed in this chapter. Travel-training that involves public transport is discussed in Chapter 8.

Importantly, when we travel-train students we need only teach a small amount at a time. The purpose of teaching is for students to learn, so we need to tailor the amount of information we give at any one time to the amount students can learn in a single session. For example, if students are walking to a shop, a route that involves two pedestrian crossings, then they might only be able to concentrate on learning at one crossing. At the next pedestrian crossing the teacher might simply role-model how to cross and allow the students to observe. When the teacher decides it is safe to cross because the cars have stopped, then all the students can cross the road as a group. It is unnecessary for each student to be shaped in this situation as they might have become restless or lost concentration. However, they will have noticed the teacher role-modeling this skill so are still continuing to learn in a way where they remain receptive and which is pleasing and positive for them.

Teachers often ask me whether using toy models in the classroom is useful for teaching travel-training skills relating to public transport. These models have included miniature cars, buses, trains, traffic lights, stop signs, pedestrian crossings, and so on, or pictures of road crossing scenarios have been used. The answer depends on your students' ability to understand these concepts. That is, if your students understand that the models replicate real-world scenarios, then use them before going out into the real world to apply the lessons. Some students benefit from watching videos of people crossing roads or taking public transport. Use whatever tool helps your students to learn best.

Regardless, there is no better way to teach students to travel than in the real world.

KEY POINTS

» The emphasis of travel-training at school is for students to learn essential foundation skills and develop self-confidence in preparation for independent travel.

» On travel-training exercises, teach students to always put on a hat or scarf in bright red, bright yellow, or bright orange to increase their visibility, and therefore safety, on the roads.

» Students build self-confidence by taking on important travel-training tasks within the school.

» At the school canteen students learn how to queue in a line, purchase items, and wait for change.

» On travel-training routes with teachers, students learn how to cross driveways and crossings, use a mobile and public phone, how to purchase items in shops, and, sometimes, how to travel on public transport.

10

Travel-Training
Case Studies

Here are nine travel-training route types for beginner, intermediate, and advanced travelers. Over the 30 years I have been teaching travel-training, these situations have presented themselves on many occasions. These travelers were between 15 and 43 years of age and had Down syndrome, autism, and intellectual disabilities. I have worked with students as young as eight to reach independence at a beginner level. Younger students (1 to 7 years) have also been taught skills, though the emphasis has not been on gaining independence but rather on confidence and skill development in readiness for future independent travel. These are real cases though all names are pseudonyms. You might find this a useful guide for your own students.

Routes for beginner travelers

CASE STUDY 1:   GREG (15 YEARS)

Previous skills: No prior travel experience

Route learned: From home to the local shop (no road crossings)

Skills learned: Using his mobile phone, independent walking, purchasing an item in a shop

Often, parents or school teachers contact me when a student who is about 15 years of age needs to travel to work experience or an extracurricular course that's a long way from school. Parents might be working or otherwise unavailable during the day and cannot drive the student to their destination. Greg was referred to me for these reasons.

Greg, typical of such students, had never walked anywhere by himself. His teacher wanted to teach him to catch a train to work experience, thinking it would only take a week or two to accomplish. This concerned me because—as you now know—Greg would have been in danger if he did not first learn important foundation skills that allowed him to travel safely, such as gaining the confidence to walk by himself, contacting his teacher once he'd arrived at his destination, and seeking help if he needed it. Greg also needed to develop traffic awareness and learn how to cross driveways safely.

When I explained this to the teacher, she arranged for Greg to be driven to work experience while we worked together to develop a travel-training program for him. We designed the following program using the five travel-training steps to develop Greg's confidence and travel skills.

1. Understanding "Who is Greg?"

Before assisting in designing this travel-training program, I needed to understand who Greg was in terms of his personality, behavior, strengths, and weaknesses. Greg had Down syndrome, was reasonably confident and healthy, could tolerate physical contact (important if the trainer needed to provide any physical prompts), and observed people and what was going on in his surroundings. He enjoyed a range of activities such as walking, swimming, football, and bowling. He enjoyed playing games on his computer, although he did not know how to use a mobile phone. He could, however, make a phone call from his home using the landline. Greg was tidy and methodical in the way he approached daily tasks such as preparing to go to school. He enjoyed routine and his behavior was never impulsive.

His speech was limited and unclear, although he understood what others were saying to him. He found it frustrating when others could not understand what he was saying, and usually avoided talking to people that he did not know and would keep to himself. He enjoyed going to DVD and computer shops, and enjoyed a particular health food bar. He had never purchased an item independently though he carried a wallet that he used at the school canteen with help. His mother was unsure whether he had money skills or knew how to buy an item in a shop. He had never crossed roads without help. He lived within walking distance of a local shop that sold groceries. He had no fear of loud noises, crowds, dogs, or other environmental variables. He was usually compliant to requests if they seemed reasonable.

2. Establishing the travel-training goal

We tailored a travel-training goal for Greg that considered his strengths and weaknesses. To keep Greg motivated on the route it was important that it had purpose to him. Given he enjoyed eating a particular health food bar, the goal of the travel-training program was for Greg to walk from home around the block of his street to the local shop where he could purchase a health bar.

This goal would enable Greg to learn how to walk confidently and independently, negotiate driveways and pedestrians, make a phone call on his mobile phone to confirm his arrival at the shop, enter a shop, and choose and purchase an item. To keep Greg motivated to want this treat, we decided that he would have it only when he purchased it himself during travel-training. If the treat was available at other times, he might lose interest in walking to the shop to buy it.

We decided to teach Greg one direction of the route at a time (from his home to the shop). There was a lot to learn on this route, and teaching the reverse route at the same time would have been too much information and too overwhelming for him. We wanted to keep training at a level where Greg could experience continual success and progress throughout the training to completion.

3. Planning the route prior to teaching

Once we had decided on the route and Greg agreed he would like to walk to the shop to buy his treat, the teacher and I walked the route to investigate what it involved. Essentially, there was one wide driveway where Greg would need to stop and look for vehicles entering and exiting, and five small driveways. We decided not to stop Greg at these smaller driveways but to observe whether he noticed cars exiting or entering them, and how he responded. Given Greg was an aware young man, methodical and not impulsive, we thought it was likely he would stop if he saw a car coming toward him. However, in the initial stages of training we would remain close to him so that we could stop him if he was in any danger on the driveways.

Outside the shop was a place where Greg could stand under shelter to phone his mother on his mobile and confirm he had arrived. This place would be out of the way of crowds and was reasonably quiet. Inside the shop, the health bar was located in an aisle close to the door. Once Greg found the treat we would teach him to take his money out of his wallet (using a paper note only) at the treat section. Using this strategy he would be able to purchase his treat quickly rather than taking a long time to manipulate coins at the cashiers' counter. To purchase the item Greg would need to queue with other customers until it was his turn to make a purchase.

In total, the route to the shop would take Greg approximately 15 minutes to walk. We broke it down into four segments that we believed would be small enough for him to learn easily:

1. from home to the corner of Banksia Street

2. from the corner of Banksia Street to the corner of Kilparra Street

3. from the corner of Kilparra Street to the shop

4. in the shop making the purchase.

The teacher and I had to decide whether we would backward chain or forward chain the route. We decided to backward chain the route, teaching the last segment first (segment 4) to keep Greg motivated and reduce the training time (a shorter training time often has greater benefits for the student in terms of remembering key training points and maintaining the motivation to participate in training).

Prior to starting travel-training the teacher introduced the mobile phone to Greg. The plan was that he would receive phone training at school by a teacher and at home by his mother. Together the mother and teacher agreed upon the phone training approach, meaning they could both teach Greg the same way. His phone had large buttons and his mother's phone number was programmed into it. To ring his mother, he simply had to press three buttons, which the teacher color coded. Color coding made it easy for Greg to remember the order in which to press the buttons (the first button was red, the second was yellow, the third was blue). When his mother answered the phone he was taught to say, "I'm at the shop," upon which his mother would praise him for arriving and ringing her.

Greg needed to increase his visibility, and therefore safety, when traveling. We taught him to develop the habit of wearing an item in one of the three safety colors. He didn't like wearing hats, so his mother gave him a yellow "travel-training backpack" in which he could carry his wallet and health bar. He kept his backpack on a hook in his bedroom.

4. Training techniques used to teach the route

During the first training session the teacher, Greg, and I walked from home to the shop. If a skill needed to be taught, I would teach it and the teacher observed. In the following sessions, she gradually took over the training and I observed her, providing any necessary feedback. Eventually she would train Greg to become independent on this route and consult with me if she needed any advice.

The first session was designed to allow Greg to observe the route to the shop. It was important to allow him to take in the environment in his own way. We expected Greg to take notice of landmarks and objects along the route that had meaning to him, which would help him become familiar with the route and to remember in which direction to go.

In this first session, we also wanted to observe his behavior so that we had a clearer understanding of exactly which skills we needed to teach (for example, did he stop at driveways; was he confident to walk in front of us; did he engage in any behaviors indicating his nervousness; did he understand how to wait in a queue until it was his turn to be served; could he get his wallet out of his bag and take out his money; could he put the change back into his wallet and place the wallet and health bar into his bag?).

During the walk to the shop we observed that Greg:

- was confident to walk about ten steps in front of us and only looked back twice to see if we were there. I gave him directions when needed: "Hey Greg, well done, you're going the right way. We can turn right here now" (pointing to the right to which Greg responded correctly by walking in the right-hand direction)

- appeared to look around him and take notice of the direction in which he was walking

- stopped at a small driveway when a car was reversing out of it

- did not stop at the other small driveways (but there were no cars exiting or entering the driveways at that time)

- hesitated at the wide driveway, looking down into it to see if any cars were coming. He did not seem to look to his left to see if cars were entering the driveway from the road.

When we arrived outside the shop I showed Greg exactly where to stand (near a wooden pole) and prompted him to take out his mobile phone to call his mother: "Greg, at this pole you can take out your phone. Come over and look at the pole with me." We both examined the pole by feeling it and talking about it. At this stage I gave him five run-throughs at using his phone and he ultimately phoned his mother independently. Once he had confirmed with his mother he had arrived, we walked into the shop.

We walked down the first aisle, located the health treat, then asked Greg to take out his money. He was out of the way of other customers and Greg could take his time and prepare methodically for his purchase. His teacher and I judged it was better to prepare early than at the cashier's counter, which would take too much time and possibly frustrate the cashier and other customers. Greg only had one paper note of a small denomination in his wallet. (When a learner is inexperienced in handling money, a single note is preferred to avoid confusion about the number of coins to use and to avoid dropping coins.)

Once Greg had the treat and his money, we approached the cashier. There were three cashiers with queues of people waiting to be served. Greg couldn't determine which queue had fewer people in it and appeared confused about queuing. To make it straightforward we joined the first queue and continued over time to teach Greg to always join the first queue. As there were people queuing in this line we observed whether Greg knew how to follow a queue and respond when it was his turn to approach the cashier—he did need a physical prompt to move ahead in the queue. After the physical prompt he moved forward and was immediately praised for moving ahead. I suggested he remain about one arm's length away from the person in front of him (we both extended our arms to check that we were about an arm's length away from the person in front of us).

When it was Greg's turn, he knew to place his item on the counter. The cashier told him the price and we prompted him to give the cashier his money. As he gave the cashier his money I immediately turned his hand over so that he could receive his change. He kept his hand extended to receive the change and I role-modeled this action by also extending mine. Once he had received the change and his item he simply dropped both into his bag and we gave him lots of praise for initiating this. I think he realized that it was too much of a bother to reach for his wallet in his bag and place the money in it. Dropping the money into his bag was a good idea and quickened the purchase process, and he could sort his money out later once he had arrived home.

Greg then left the shop and was excited that he was on his way home to eat his favorite treat.

Importantly:

- Throughout this training process we only spoke to Greg when we were teaching him a skill or providing praise when he completed a desired task or action.

- At the conclusion of the training session (segment 4: in-shop purchase), we walked home without actively training Greg, encouraging him to walk about ten steps in front of us which he did happily. At the wide driveway I role-modeled the correct action of looking both ways for vehicles while Greg observed (and learned). The emphasis was on me doing the task, taking the pressure and expectation off Greg. He had achieved enough for one day. Once he arrived home he quickly took out his health bar and sat down to enjoy his well-earned treat.

From this first session, we learned that the specific skills Greg needed to learn on segment 4 of the route were: walking from home in the direction of the shop; consistently stopping and looking both ways for vehicles at the wide driveway; stopping at the smaller driveways when a car approached him; stopping at the wooden pole at the shop and to phone his mother; walking to the health bar; taking out his money; walking back down the first aisle toward the first cashier queue; joining the queue, keeping approximately an arm's length away from the person in front of him; moving forward in the queue when needed; when it was his turn, placing the health bar on the counter and presenting the money to the cashier; waiting for change with his hand open and extended; taking the change and health bar and dropping them in his bag; exiting the shop.

The most effective way of teaching these skills, as discussed in previous chapters, is through repetition and reinforcement. When Greg began to initiate and demonstrate these skills consistently, then it was time to let him do these without prompts of any kind. The trainers might even move away from him by about five steps. When Greg initiated all of these skills and we believed he could do each of them independently, then it was time to commence fading out from this program.

5. Fading out and allowing the student to travel independently

When we observed Greg from a short distance away ringing his mother to confirm his arrival at the shop, entering the shop, and carrying out each step in the purchase procedure, it was time to set the fading-out criteria to test whether or not Greg really had developed the skills to consistently succeed on this part of the route.

We set an initial performance criterion of eight successful purchasing procedures and observed Greg from about 20 paces, once a week over eight weeks. When we began to fade out we didn't move too far away, just in case we needed to intervene or retrain an aspect of the route. If we moved too far away it could have been demotivating for both Greg and the teacher to have to come back together again from a great distance to retrain. Fading out gradually provided a successful and motivating experience for the student and trainer.

If, during the eight-week observation period, Greg experienced difficulty, we would not have immediately rushed in to assist him. Instead, we would have given him time to see if he could problem solve the situation. After all, he had been training on this section of the route for a number of weeks and might have learned additional coping skills that were not immediately evident. If there was a difficulty he could not solve, such as forgetting his money and being unable to pay for his treat at the counter, then this would have been a terrific training opportunity. We might have approached Greg and explained that without money he could not purchase the item. Instead, he would have to return home to get his money and walk back again. (Greg probably would not have been happy, but I bet he would never have forgotten his money in future!) If we were required to intervene, say, on the fifth observation of eight, then we would have had to start the criteria again from observation 1. Although this might seem time consuming, it allows valuable time to observe and possibly train for most situations that might arise.

Once we observed Greg succeed eight consecutive times, it was time to move back further, about 40 paces. We then set a criterion of four times. Once Greg succeeded four consecutive times, then we moved away to the shop's entry door. It was important that Greg could still see us at this point, even if he appeared confident and able. Probably his self-confidence would have been quite high, although if he did experience a difficulty he could lose confidence very quickly without praise and possible intervention. From the door we observed him another eight times. Once successful, we informed Greg that we would wait outside the shop for him. We were still able to subtly observe Greg to check that his confidence and behavior was maintained when he thought we were not there.

When the trainer fades out gradually it is unusual that a change in student behavior occurs, but it can happen. Again we set a criterion of eight times. Once Greg achieved this, we confidently assumed that he was now independent on segment 4 of the route. Importantly, we not only trained Greg but also observed him on the route independently, without intervention, approximately 20 times.

We then trained on segment 3 of the route, from the corner of Kilparra Street to the shop. On this section there was a wide driveway. Again, through repetition and positive reinforcement, we taught Greg to stop, look both ways for traffic, wave traffic on if it appeared, and walk across the driveway once clear. Because we had already walked the route over many weeks Greg already knew what to do in the shop at the end of segment 3.

When we believed Greg was independent on segment 3 of the route we set a criterion. As a guideline, the riskier the situation the higher you should set the criterion. In this section of the route there was the driveway. Therefore, we moved away about 15 paces and observed Greg on this section about ten times. Once Greg arrived at the shop, he was independent so we left him to do this in-shop process on his own. We simply waited outside.

Once Greg succeeded on segment 3 of the route, we moved further away and observed another ten times. We repeated this process until we were observing Greg from a considerable distance. During the final observation criterion, we walked a long distance ahead of Greg and met him at the shop.

Once we faded out from segment 3, we then taught segment 2, from the corner of Banksia Street to the corner of Kilparra Street. We repeated the teaching and fade-out process until Greg was walking from home to the shop independently. Because Greg had yet to learn to travel the route from the shop to home we needed to continue meeting him outside the shop. After a few months we commenced teaching the route from the shop back home.

CASE STUDY 2:   STEVE (17 YEARS)

Previous skills: No prior travel experience

Route learned: From the stairs in the local mall to the game shop (and return)

Skills learned: Using his mobile phone, independent walking, and back-up strategies

Steve's mother, Bridget, contacted me, believing he was ready for travel-training as all other aspects of his life appeared to be going well. She had wanted Steve to learn travel-training skills at a younger age but believed he was not emotionally ready, as he often did not want to leave the house. At the age of 15 he was homeschooled for about eight months because he refused to go to school. At the recommendation of a teacher, Steve—who enjoyed playing video games online—joined an online gaming group and over time made friends with two other boys his own age. This proved to be a turning point and Steve became increasingly receptive to other activities and people. He eventually agreed to return to school. Steve had never traveled anywhere independently and Bridget wanted him to learn safe travel skills in anticipation of traveling to post-school employment and other activities.

1. Understanding "Who is Steve?"

When I met Steve he was attending school regularly and was doing well, particularly in math and science. He enjoyed his home routine, reading books about planes, and playing video games and competing online against friends. He often won and would proudly declare these wins to his parents. Steve had autism and particularly disliked being in crowds, the cries of babies, and being touched. When faced with any of these he would rock back and forth in an agitated state, flap his hands, and talk loudly about how noisy it was. He had not learned strategies to deal with these aversive situations.

Steve was able to read the time using both digital and analog clocks. He was talented with technology and could teach himself to use devices. He would frequently repair mobile phones for his parents. He would disassemble items, analyze the problem and fix it, and reassemble the device. If he was unable to solve a problem, then he usually knew why and would communicate this to his parents. He used his mobile phone to text and use apps, though avoided talking on the phone. He was familiar with his local community although he had never traveled anywhere by himself.

2. Establishing the travel-training goal

Steve lived a long distance from shops that could only be reached by crossing roads. In these situations, I often arrange for students to be driven or accompanied to local shops or a mall and, from a point near the shop or in the mall, taught a route to a shop of their choice. This way the student learns to walk to a location independently, back-up strategies that will assist in difficult situations, to negotiate pedestrians, to purchase an item, and thereby build self-confidence.

Upon discussion with Steve about a travel-training goal, the only shop he wanted to go to was the video games (gaming) shop at the local mall. He rarely went there but knew all the latest games, having researched them online, and was keen to see the actual games in the shop. His mother agreed they could visit the shop on Saturdays to look at the games, and once a month he could purchase one game. This proposal was highly motivating to Steve despite his ambivalence about crowds and babies.

We decided that Bridget would drive Steve to the mall. The goal of the program was that, upon entering the mall, Bridget would wait at the bottom of the stairs and Steve would walk to the game shop—a ten-minute walk from the stairs. He would phone his mother to tell her he had arrived, spend 20 minutes in the shop, and then return to his mother.

3. Planning the route prior to teaching

To investigate what was involved in this route, Bridget and I met (without Steve) at the mall at the bottom of the stairs and walked through the route together. We walked up the stairs to level 1, then past fashion shops and noisy crowded cafés with outdoor eating areas, and eventually reached the gaming shop. Along the route there were some comfortable lounges in relatively quiet locations. The gaming shop was large, with plenty of space to move about. The shop seemed to attract people in their late teens and twenties. Outside the shop was a quiet seating area where Steve could text his mother using his mobile phone to let her know that he had arrived.

Bridget and I decided to forward chain this route (that is, to teach the route from the beginning to the end) in one segment because the route was fairly short and Steve was highly motivated to visit the games shop. Also, he was very intelligent and learned quickly so it was not necessary to break the route into small learning segments.

The main skills that Steve needed to learn were back-up strategies to cope with the noise and crowds that would agitate him along the route. We decided that Steve would take his phone earphones on the route to help him cope, and a plane magazine. The earphones reduced external noise to a considerable extent and he could use them if the noise in the mall became too disturbing. We would also encourage him to sit in the quiet seating areas if the crowds became too overwhelming for him en route to the gaming shop. He could also read his plane magazine, which usually helped him feel calm. Once he felt calm he could continue on his way to the shop. Importantly, although he was traveling inside a mall, he would be encouraged to wear his red hat. Forming the habit of wearing the hat before leaving home was important preparation for future travel-training in outdoor environments where being highly visible to vehicles would be essential for safe travel.

4. Training techniques used to teach the route

Before commencing the first session with Steve, at home his mother explained that we would be walking to the gaming shop and he could look at the games for 20 minutes. She also explained that if it was noisy in the mall, then he could use his earphones to make it quieter and also sit in some "quiet chairs." While in the quiet chairs he could read his plane magazine to help him feel calm again. When he felt calm, he could continue walking to the games shop.

At the mall the three of us walked the route together so Steve could observe the direction of the gaming shop from the stairs. As we walked past the cafés, Steve began to feel agitated. At this point his mother encouraged him to use his earphones, which he did. His mother then pointed out the quiet chairs and explained he could sit in these anytime he wanted to help himself feel calm. Steve then walked over to a quiet chair and sat down. He took from his bag a plane magazine and began reading it. After about five minutes he said he was ready to go to the gaming shop and he appeared visibly calmer and keen to move on.

When Steve arrived at the gaming shop, his mother showed him the seats outside the shop where he could sit and text her to let her know he had arrived. She invited him to text her but Steve declined, explaining she was already with him so there was no need. Bridget then explained that he could go into the shop and look around for 20 minutes, after which he could meet us back at the seats. Steve went into the shop and returned 20 minutes later and appeared to have enjoyed his time. Bridget then asked him to take us back to the stairs. He knew the direction and walked very quickly back to the stairs. He did stop to put his headphones in without any prompt and we praised him. Once we arrived at the stairs Steve appeared pleased and talked excitedly about the games he saw in the shop.

In later training sessions Steve began initiating putting in the earphones and sitting down when he needed to feel calm again. Bridget began walking a few meters behind him on the route without interacting with him. When Bridget believed he was traveling the route without prompts of any kind, she then commenced fading out from this program.

5. Fading out and allowing the student to travel independently

To be confident that Steve could consistently travel the route and apply the earphone and seating strategies, Bridget set the fading-out performance criteria.

- She initially observed Steve once a week over five weeks, walking about 4 meters (13 feet) behind him. During these weeks Steve consistently used his earphone/seating strategy when he needed to and texted her when he arrived at the gaming shop.

- She then observed him once a week for another five weeks, following 10 meters (33 feet) behind. Again he consistently applied his coping strategies.

- After this she moved away to where she could see Steve, but he could not see her, and observed him once a week for another three weeks. Again Steve applied the techniques we had taught him.

- Finally, Bridget told Steve she would wait at the stairs while he went to the games shop and he could return to the stairs once he had finished, which he did.

By the end of training Steve was applying these coping techniques at the mall and at other times in his life. He used them at school and when in public. He appeared calmer and more confident knowing he had some control over his environment. Steve had learned some vital foundation skills and moved on to learn travel routes at an intermediate level. For example, Bridget began driving him to a local shop where he learned to cross at traffic lights and go into the shop to make a purchase. He could independently apply the coping techniques we taught him, though instead of a "quiet chair" there were "quiet places" along the route where he could stop and collect himself when he felt the need.

CASE STUDY 3:   SARA (12 YEARS)

Previous skills: No prior travel experience

Route learned: From the car park into the bowling alley

Skills learned: Using her mobile phone, vehicle awareness, and stranger danger

Sara's mother, Eileen, wanted her to become more independent in preparation for travel-training to high school the following year. Sara was very confident and frequently talked to people she didn't know when she was out with the school or her family. She had not developed vehicle awareness as she was usually told when to stop for vehicles and when to go, and had never walked anywhere by herself. Therefore, before more complex travel-training programs could be undertaken, Sara needed to develop "stranger danger" strategies, understand vehicle safety, and learn to use a mobile phone.

1. Understanding "Who is Sara?"

Sara had an intellectual disability, was very social, and enjoyed interacting with people regardless of whether she knew them. She had various interests such as bowling, swimming, painting, listening to music, and dancing, and often met friends on weekends. Sara liked talking on the phone with friends and knew how to use her home telephone, although had yet to learn to use a mobile phone. She disliked using a computer or any other technology and grew impatient if she could not acquire a skill quickly. She was flexible and casual and did not follow a routine at home.

2. Establishing the travel-training goal

Upon the suggestion of learning to travel by herself, Sara was excited and wanted to learn how to get to many places to meet her friends. After discussion with her mother, she decided her top priority was learning to meet her friends at the bowling alley where she bowled every second weekend. Because she had little awareness of vehicles and had never walked anywhere independently, Eileen and I decided that she would avoid crossing roads at this early stage, and that Eileen would drive her to a couple of hundred meters away from the bowling alley, and she would walk into the bowling alley from her mother's car.

3. Planning the route prior to teaching

Eileen and I met near the bowling alley to review the route. Eileen could park in a nearby outdoor shopping center car park where Sara would need to walk through an outdoor café, cross two small driveways, and walk up a hill to the bowling alley. Just inside the door of the bowling alley was a small reception area where Sara could ring Eileen to let her know she had arrived. Sara was fond of wearing yellow so it was decided she could wear any item of bright yellow she liked on the bowling day, for example, a yellow bag, shirt, or scarf.

Eileen and I decided to backward chain this route to reduce the training time and reduce the likelihood of Sara getting frustrated if she found some of the route difficult or confronting. Although this route seems short, there were some significant lessons in it for Sara, such as not initiating conversation with strangers, which she usually enjoyed doing; watching for vehicles on driveways; and learning to use her mobile phone. Therefore, the route was broken down into three segments, namely:

1. from the car to the café

2. from the café to the first driveway

3. from the first driveway to the reception area of the bowling alley (including a second driveway).

The last segment (3) of the route would be taught first: from the first driveway to the reception area of the bowling alley (including a second driveway).

Because Sara was skilled at matching, it was decided that she would carry a small pocket telephone book with her mother's phone number in it that she could use when ringing on her mobile phone. She could also use her painting skills to beautify the phone book, which would motivate Sara to take the book with her.

4. Training techniques used to teach the route

The first training session involved Eileen, Sara, and me walking from the first driveway into the reception area of the bowling alley. Eileen parked her car near the first driveway rather than in the shopping center car park—if she had parked in the car park then Sara would have stopped to talk to people in the café on the way past, and we wanted to avoid this in the early stages of the training. We wanted Sara to learn the last segment of the route first—this was already complex enough, and we didn't want to overwhelm her or make travel-training a negative experience.

At the first driveway a car was entering from the road. Eileen and I were an arm's length away from Sara. We didn't tell Sara what to do but observed her reaction to the car. Sara saw the car but went to walk across the driveway in front of it. This was an ideal training opportunity. I gently stopped Sara by placing my hand in front of her shoulder and pointed to the car. Sara and I waved the car on, encouraging the driver into the driveway. I calmly told Sara that when there is a car, we stop. Then we walked to the second driveway. At this driveway there were no cars entering or exiting. However, because Sara needed to learn to always look on driveways, we needed to formalize this looking process. I gently stopped Sara, pointed in one direction, then in the other, and said, "No cars—we can walk." The expectation for the future is that Sara does not necessarily stop at every driveway but do as we do—scan before reaching the driveway or even use hearing or peripheral vision to judge when it's safe to cross. Whatever technique she uses to cross a driveway is irrelevant, but the point is she must become aware that vehicles might be entering or exiting a driveway and respond appropriately.

From the second driveway we walked to the reception area of the bowling alley. Here, I prompted Sara to take out her telephone book and locate her mother's mobile phone number. Eileen waited outside. Sara matched each number with the number in the phone book and rang her mother's phone. When Eileen answered she gave Sara a lot of praise for dialing correctly and arriving safely.

Importantly:

- Throughout training we only spoke to Sara to teach her a skill or provide her with praise when she completed a desired action or task.

- On the return route to the car, Sara walked a meter or two (6 feet) in front of us. At the driveways, Eileen role-modeled looking for cars while Sara stood beside her. We noticed Sara observing her mother, which was an effective way for Sara to learn.

- We used repetition and reinforcement to teach the skills on this route. When Sara began to initiate and demonstrate that she could—consistently and without prompts—stop and look for vehicles and identify when it was safe to cross, and phone her mother, it was time for Eileen to move about 2 meters (6 feet) away from Sara. When Eileen continued to observe Sara reacting and behaving appropriately without prompting it was time to fade out from this segment of the route.

5. Fading out and allowing the student to travel independently

To observe if Sara could consistently travel this section of the route independently, Eileen set a fading-out criterion.

- First, Eileen required Sara to ring from the reception area while she waited outside, once a week for five consecutive weeks.

- Once Sara had accomplished this, Eileen then waited about 10 meters (32 feet) away from the bowling alley once a week for three weeks.

- After this Eileen waited on the other side of the second driveway once a week for five weeks while Sara continued to the bowling alley.

- Finally, Eileen waited at the first driveway and observed Sara cross this driveway independently and walk to the bowling alley eight times.

Once Sara had completed the fade-out process she was deemed independent on segment 3 and training commenced on segment 2 (from the café area to the first driveway). Once she had reached the first driveway, Sara would walk the rest of the way independently as she had learned segment 3 of the route.

Stranger danger awareness

Segment 2 of the route was challenging for Sara, as she was required to learn some "stranger danger" strategies. Sara frequently initiated conversation with strangers, which is considered unsafe because it might place her in a vulnerable situation in the future when she learns to travel on public transport during the day, and possibly at night. It is very difficult to completely stop behaviors that occur so naturally in older children, especially when they appear to be a genuine part of their personality. It is far easier to shape a child's behavior in the early years. To change behavior in an older child the trainer needs to think of an appropriate way that will be accepted by the student. For Sara, we devised a couple of successful strategies. First, Sara's mother explained why we only initiate conversation with people we know; and if people we do not know ask us a question, we then say, "I don't know," and move away from that person. Second, Eileen showed Sara a video that also explained and demonstrated the way we treat and react to strangers. Sara was allowed to keep the video and play it whenever she wished. Third, as Sara loved music, she listened to music through earphones on the way to the bowling alley. This was enjoyable for Sara and also served to distract her from talking to people at the café. She learned to keep the music at a low volume so that she could still hear vehicles entering/ exiting the driveways. Finally, at school, Sara and her classmates did role-modeling about stranger danger, which also helped to reinforce how to react to strangers. These activities included a clear explanation and role-modeling that if Sara needed help, she could either call her mother on the phone, approach a café staff member, or ask a lady with a pram. I realize "a lady with a pram" is a stereotype of a safe person, but this genuinely seems to be the case.

On segment 2 of the route Eileen parked near the café. Eileen and Sara walked through the café area to the first driveway. Eileen taught this section of the route, including the stranger danger strategy, while using repetitive training and positive reinforcement. When Eileen believed that Sara was able to travel this section of the route without intervention, she commenced the fade-out procedure. She applied the fade-out criteria slowly, as she did in the previous route segment.

Once Sara had achieved traveling segment 2 independently, Eileen commenced training on segment 1 (from the car park to the café). She used a safe walkway from the car park so that Sara avoided moving vehicles. Wearing a bright yellow shirt and, on some days, carrying her bright orange backpack, helped vehicle drivers to see Sara, which increased her safety when walking through the car park. Once Eileen had taught and faded out from segment 1, Sara was able to travel the entire route independently. Eileen could leave Sara at the car park knowing that she would walk safely to the bowling alley and ring her on arrival. After four months of Sara traveling the route independently, Eileen met her at the bowling alley and taught her the return route back to the car park.

Routes for intermediate travelers

CASE STUDY 4:   LISA (26 YEARS)

Previous skills: Could travel two beginner routes independently

Route learned: From home to the shop with two traffic light crossings, and the return journey

Skills learned: Crossing at traffic lights and back-up strategies for when the lights are not working

Lisa lived with her father, Tim. Tim drove Lisa to and from work three days a week. Lisa wanted to learn how to travel to work by herself using public transport, but first she needed to learn to cross roads safely. This was an important prerequisite skill before taking public transport as inevitably she would need to cross roads along the route to work. Previously she had learned two beginner routes and was now confident walking alone, able to use a mobile phone independently, knew how to seek help if she needed it, and was confident purchasing one to three items in a shop. Although Lisa didn't understand the value of money, she could easily hand money to a cashier and keep her hand out to receive the change.

I had worked with Lisa and her father four years previously, but it was still important to follow each of the five steps of the teaching process. Lisa might have changed in some way, for example, developed a medical issue or a fear of some type, so it was very important to still consider "Who is Lisa?"

1. Understanding "Who is Lisa?"

Lisa had Down syndrome, was a quiet person with a soft voice, and was not fond of dogs. She had previously learned to use the "avoid dog" strategy whenever she encountered a dog in public. That is, she took slow deep breaths that helped calm her and, with elbows bent and arms tucked onto her chest, turned her back on the dog and waited until it walked past before she continued on. If she felt particularly fearful then she would do this action while continuing to walk along the path away from the dog.

Lisa was motivated to learn a route to the shop as she enjoyed purchasing items for Tim. Tim had taken photographs of food items they often ate at home that Lisa could buy at the shop. In a plastic folder Lisa kept photos of the particular bread, milk, and fruit they enjoyed and a favorite type of biscuit. Before going to the shop Lisa would pack two or three photos of the items she planned to buy, and refer to those photos once in the shop to remind her which items she needed to purchase. She was happy to purchase up to three items at a time. The number of items would increase over time, but only when she felt ready to do this. Tim would always suggest they needed a particular two or three items that day—though on occasions would also suggest it would be good to have some biscuits, too, if she wanted to buy them as well. If Lisa said no then that was fine.

Lisa had a particular cupboard in her bedroom that contained her "travel-training" clothes. She liked wearing red and orange, and had a range of shirts and dresses in these colors. As part of her "going to the shop" preparation she would pack her wallet, photos, and mobile phone, and would dress in one of these safety items. She also had a folding red umbrella in case it rained, and always kept it in her bag.

2. Establishing the travel-training goal

We wanted to teach Lisa to cross at traffic lights so planned a route specifically to include these. There was a small grocery shop about a 20-minute walk from Lisa's home that required her to cross two sets of traffic lights. She usually walked this route with her father to purchase a few items each week, and she enjoyed this task very much.

Lisa had learned two beginner routes previously which she was still traveling, so her confidence in her ability to travel was high. Because of this, in the new travel-training program, we decided to teach Lisa the return route as well as the route to the shop.

3. Planning the route prior to teaching

Tim and I walked the route to investigate what it actually involved. We walked the route at the same time of day that Lisa would walk it to observe the amount of traffic and pedestrians at that time. We did not rush, but allowed plenty of time to observe the "behavior" of the traffic as well as environmental factors such as the positioning of the sun and whether or not it interfered with the driver's vision, mainly because of the glare if they were driving into the sun. In the morning rush hour, and in the afternoon when drivers are returning home, they often take more risks or drive faster. These factors determined the level of caution that Lisa needed to take, and affected the way we taught her this route.

On the route Lisa needed to cross two large driveways that were the entry and exit points to a large business center and an apartment block. She also needed to cross roads at two sets of traffic lights. The larger of these crossings was across four lanes of traffic and the smaller one was across two lanes of traffic. On the larger crossing we observed large trucks as well as cars traveling on the road. This was an important observation because it meant that Lisa would need to stand behind the traffic light pole in case a truck turned the corner too closely to Lisa and the truck's wheel mounted the pedestrian walkway. Although this seems unlikely, I have seen similar incidents occur many times.

We also noticed that near both sets of traffic lights were large signal boxes which control the speed of the traffic lights and are also where repairs take place if the lights break down. (In Australia, written on the outside of the box is a four-digit number which indicates the location of each set of lights: for example, at the corner of Jersey Street and Palm Street, in the suburb of Glebe. Also written on the box is a telephone number. If the traffic lights are not working, then a member of the public can phone the number and report that the lights are broken, quoting the four-digit identification number on the box. Usually, the local council responsible for maintaining traffic lights will repair these within a day or two.) It was important to teach Lisa to tell her father when the lights were out of order so they could report this to the council and have them repaired. If the lights were not working, then Lisa also needed to be taught a back-up strategy so that she could get across the road safely.

The route to the shop would take Lisa about 20 minutes to walk. Outside the shop was a quiet area where she could phone her father to let him know she had arrived. Because Lisa had been to the shop numerous times previously, she was familiar with the layout, and how to queue at the cashier's counter to purchase her items. She was independent on the in-shop purchase procedure, so this section of the route did not need to be taught.

Tim and I decided to forward chain the route because it was familiar to Lisa (even though she had not traveled it independently). She was also highly motivated to travel independently and had a high level of self-confidence and ability to cope with the demands of the route.

We agreed to break the route to the shop and home again into four segments:

1. from home to the second set of traffic lights

2. from the second set of traffic lights to the shop

3. from the shop to the first set of traffic lights

4. from the first set of traffic lights to home.

4. Training techniques used to teach the route

Tim, Lisa, and I walked to the shop together to observe Lisa on this route as well as to commence teaching her. Tim and I had never observed Lisa cross at traffic lights, although when she was at school she had been on outings with other students and they often crossed at traffic lights together. Lisa might have acquired some skills from her school days, but we needed to see for ourselves if this was actually the case.

During the walk to and from the shop we observed that:

- Lisa was excited about walking to the shop and happily walked ahead of us.

- At the first driveway, she looked for vehicles and at the second driveway she stopped to allow a car to exit the driveway. The driver stopped and waved at Lisa, encouraging her to cross in front of him. Lisa, however, waved the driver on, and she crossed after he had driven away. This "waving the driver on" skill had been taught in the "beginner" programs.

- Lisa walked to the first set of traffic lights. She pressed the button and stood near the pole to wait for the green walk light. At this point I suggested to Lisa that she take a step back just behind the pole. I explained that this was the "safe place." Without hesitation she stepped into the position and Tim and I praised her for doing so.

- These lights were ATS, which emitted a quick beeping sound when it was safe to cross. As soon as the ATS sounded Lisa was about to walk across the road. Although this was the correct action for her to take, it was also an important moment to teach her to wait and count to three before crossing the road. Counting to three before crossing allows time for drivers who might speed through red lights to pass. (We used the method of counting to three because Lisa was able to do this. However, if your student cannot count then they might learn a rhythm by tapping a foot or their leg three times despite not recognizing the rhythm as "three taps.") Once Lisa had counted to three and started walking across the road, we immediately praised her (positive reinforcement). Once Lisa had walked to the other side and toward the second set of traffic lights, I prompted her to use the same "count to three" strategy at these lights.

- At the next set of lights she pressed the button independently. As before, I reminded her to stand next to the pole (which was at a distance from the curb). When the lights sounded again, I blocked her from walking by gently placing my hand in front of her shoulder (I was standing behind her) and said, "Let's count to three: 1, 2, 3." As soon as she took that first step across the road after counting Tim and I praised her, congratulating her for "standing in the safe place next to the pole and counting to three before walking."

- Lisa then walked to the shop. At the shop we showed her the quiet location outside where she could phone Tim to let him know she had arrived. I asked Lisa if she wanted to ring her father and she agreed. Tim walked away from the shop so that Lisa could not see him when she rang. Lisa confirmed she had arrived and then put her phone in her bag.

- I explained that she could now go and purchase her items and Tim and I would wait outside. When Lisa returned, the items were packed neatly in her bag and we congratulated her. She appeared pleased.

- We then walked the return route home and repeated the teaching steps that we'd applied while walking to the shop. Importantly, we only spoke to Lisa to teach her the pole positioning and to count to three, and to praise her immediately after she had performed these skills.

- When Lisa arrived home Tim summarized how well she had done and she was given some time to play her music and relax (a secondary reinforcer).

5. Fading out and allowing the student to travel independently

As Lisa and Tim continued training, Lisa began to initiate skills without being prompted, such as standing beside the pole instead of nearer to the curb and counting to three before crossing. As soon as Tim observed this occurring consistently over about four weeks, he concluded that Lisa had acquired these skills. But, instead of assuming that Lisa was now independent and able to travel to the shop, to be absolutely confident, Tim had to test his theory by setting performance criteria and slowly fading out.

Tim set a criterion of ten times (i.e. once a week for 10 weeks) to observe Lisa at the traffic lights, standing about ten steps away from her. (This might seem like a very high criterion, but the rule of thumb is to set a higher criterion if a section of the route is complex and potentially dangerous. Crossing a four-lane highway at traffic lights fits this description. The trainer needs to feel confident that the student can perform this skill independently.)

Once Tim had observed Lisa achieve the criterion, he moved further away from her at the traffic lights to about 20 paces and observed her another ten times. On observation 8, the traffic lights were not working. This was a good training opportunity, as lights breaking down would inevitably happen again at some stage. Tim approached Lisa and explained the problem. He taught her that if the lights weren't working she was to go into the nearby shop and ask for help to cross the road. Tim decided that Lisa asking a cashier for help was safer than her following another pedestrian who might rush across the road and take greater risks. This was also a reliable strategy because there were always at least two cashiers in the shop. After this explanation Lisa walked into a shop and asked for help to cross the road. Tim moved away so that the cashier did not know that he and Lisa were related. The cashier came out of the shop with Lisa and accompanied her safely across the road. (This strategy was effective for Lisa, though trainers need to problem solve what strategies might work in particular situations with their students.)

Because Tim intervened in the fade-out process, the criterion returned to zero, and he observed her crossing the road independently another ten times.

Overall, Tim took the following steps in the fading-out process, keeping in mind the segments of the route:

Segment 1: Home to the second set of traffic lights (criterion was ten times independently)

- Tim told Lisa he would meet her just after she crossed the final set of traffic lights. It was very important that Lisa did not see Tim anywhere on the route before the meeting point so that she believed she was walking independently. The advantage of this was that Tim could observe Lisa to see how she coped walking the route "alone": what she did if people talked to her; what she did if a dog appeared; whether she applied the methods of travel that he had taught her; and what she did if any other circumstances arose.

  (I recommend that when you are following a student without their knowledge, wear dark clothes, walk some distance behind on the other side of the road, use a monocular (see glossary) so that you can observe them at a greater distance, and/or drive your car and stop at various places to observe how they travel. I have used all of these methods effectively depending on the requirements of the route.)

- Once Lisa had met this criterion she was considered independent on segment 1 so from this point on, Tim met her at the final set of lights without following her.

Segment 2: From the second set of lights to the shop (criterion was three times independently)

- Tim set a criterion of Lisa traveling this section three times with no assistance. This was a low-level criterion, as segment 2 was considered to be low risk with no road crossings, and Lisa already walked similar types of routes independently. Lisa did not see Tim on this section of the route. Instead, he met her at the shop after she rang him to confirm her arrival.

- Once Lisa had achieved this criterion, she was independent on segments 1 and 2 of the route and Tim would only meet her at the shop after she had rung him to let him know she had arrived. As before, Tim had to either walk or drive to the shop without Lisa noticing him to ensure she was walking these segments independently.

Segment 3 (return journey): From the shop to the first set of traffic lights (criterion was ten times independently)

- Tim approached this segment of the route in same way as segment 1 (from home to the second set of lights). When Lisa came out of the shop, Tim told her he would meet her after the first set of traffic lights. Again, Tim avoided being seen by Lisa but could observe her along the route. During the observation period, the traffic lights had once again broken down. Lisa waited at the lights, observed that they were broken, and walked into a shop to seek help, which demonstrated she had learned a key back-up strategy. The cashier accompanied her across the road. Once Lisa had achieved independence on this segment of the route Tim faded out from the final segment.

Segment 4 (return journey): From the first traffic lights to home (criterion was three times independently)

- Lisa was now leaving home, walking to the shop independently, and meeting her father only at the first set of traffic lights on her way home (segments 1, 2, and 3). Tim was confident in Lisa, as he had observed her perform the route independently many times over the fading-out process. Lisa was also ringing him once she arrived at the shop.

- Tim met Lisa at the first set of lights after she had crossed them on the way home, and told her he would meet her at home (Lisa had her own house key and could let herself inside when she arrived). Tim observed Lisa from across the road at a great distance. Once she had arrived home three times independently he concluded that Lisa could now travel the entire route independently, without being observed.

Note that during the fade-out process Lisa had traveled the route by herself approximately 90 times, only being observed at a distance. As Lisa was traveling the route only once a week, this route took nearly two years for her to travel independently. Although this seems a long time, Lisa had acquired permanent skills, such as crossing at traffic lights and coping in busy environments, that she could apply on other routes. The likelihood of her making risky errors was very small given that she had demonstrated her skills 90 times successfully. Putting extra time into the fading-out process was essential, especially for a higher-risk route where additional challenges might arise, such as the broken traffic lights.

CASE STUDY 5:   ADNAN (27 YEARS)

Previous skills: Could travel two beginner routes independently, and two intermediate routes that included traffic lights

Route learned: Walk from his aunt's home to work

Skills learned: A longer walking route that includes pedestrian crossings

I had worked with Adnan and his family about two years prior to this training. At that stage I worked with his father, who taught him two routes that involved crossing roads at traffic lights. One of those routes was walking from home to Adnan's workplace where he worked two days a week. Recently, Adnan's workplace had relocated three suburbs away (about a 20-minute car trip). His workplace required him to travel at least part of the route to/from work independently.

Although Adnan was a confident traveler and had developed a range of skills (vehicle awareness, using a mobile phone, seeking help if required, crossing at traffic lights safely), he still had to learn more complex road crosses and travel for longer periods to increase his self-confidence before learning to travel on public transport. Fortunately, Adnan's aunt (Salma) lived close to his workplace and the family decided that, for two days a week, he would stay with her and walk to and from work. Adnan had stayed overnight with his aunt over the years and was familiar with the local area where she lived.

Even though I had worked with Adnan previously, it was still important that I gathered some information about "who Adnan is today" in case his situation, behavior, or likes/dislikes had changed in any way.

1. Understanding "Who is Adnan?"

Adnan had autism and an intellectual disability, and was tactile defensive—that is, he disliked being touched or touching textures. He was a quiet person, although he would greet people he knew when he arrived home. Once there, he would avoid further communication with people by looking away. He also tried to complete tasks quickly if the task involved another person. Adnan enjoyed the routine and familiarity of going to work and was happy to be involved in the training from his aunt's home to work. However, he had a strong dislike for walking in the rain and could not tolerate using an umbrella. If he had to walk in the rain, then he would prefer to run to his destination and would become exhausted.

2. Establishing the travel-training goal

The route from Salma's home to work was lengthy and involved a 2-kilometer walk (1.5 miles), crossing at a set of traffic lights and two pedestrian crossings. There was a shorter route through a park that would prevent Adnan having to cross at the pedestrian crossings but we decided this route was too isolated, and possibly risky. Also, given Adnan disliked rain it was important that the route include areas where he could stop and shelter if he wished. Because Adnan was a relatively experienced traveler we decided to teach him the route to and from work on the same day. That is, his aunt would teach him how to travel to work in the morning, and then meet him in the afternoon to teach him the route home.

3. Planning the route prior to teaching

Salma and I walked the morning and afternoon routes at similar times to those that Adnan would be walking to or from work. This helped us assess the amount of vehicle and pedestrian traffic Adnan would be exposed to, as well as driver behavior at the two pedestrian crossings. Along the route we also located sheltered places near shops, in two bus shelters, and in thick tree foliage where Adnan could stop to avoid the rain if he wished.

The two pedestrian crossings varied significantly from each other. One crossing was located near the shops with frequent traffic flow. The road was wide, though there was a traffic island in the middle dividing the crossing into two sections. The other crossing was on a narrower road with less traffic; however, both sides had tree branches and shrubs extending onto the crossing blocking the pedestrian and driver's ability to see clearly. The conditions of both pedestrian crossings influenced where we wanted to position Adnan when preparing to cross these roads.

Because Adnan was motivated to travel this route and was an experienced and relatively confident traveler, we decided to forward chain the route and divided it into only two segments:

1. from home to the shops

2. from the shops to the workplace.

4. Training techniques used to teach the route

Adnan, Salma, and I walked the route to work. Along the way we pointed out the sheltered locations to Adnan where he could stop to avoid the rain—or for a brief rest—if he wished. On this particular day the weather was overcast with possibilities of rain. Adnan prepared by wearing his yellow raincoat—a preferred color as it increased his visibility to drivers, thereby increasing his safety when crossing roads.

Adnan had never crossed a pedestrian crossing independently. When he approached the busy crossing we observed that he stopped a meter or two behind the marked crossing, with the result that vehicles did not stop for him. After waiting about five minutes, Adnan did not change his position and began to look a little unsure of what to do.

At this point I intervened, not wanting the experience to become a negative one. I repositioned Adnan in a safe and highly visible position where he placed one foot on the crossing. I modeled a "get ready to walk" position (a side-on body position with one foot in front and one foot behind) which he copied, alerting drivers to his intention to cross the road. Because there was an island in the middle of the road Adnan needed only to look in one direction to ensure there were no cars or that the cars had stopped before he crossed. Taking my position behind Adnan I simply said, "When the cars stop you can walk." (Because this crossing was very busy there would always be cars traveling along this road at the time Adnan was walking.) Adnan might not have understood this instruction but that did not matter. With training and repetition, he would eventually understand the pattern of what to do. Seeing Adnan's position on the pedestrian crossing, a car stopped. I immediately pointed to the car and said, "The car has stopped," and gently nudged Adnan forward so that he began walking across to the island in the middle of the road. As soon as he took the first step I said, "Great Adnan—the car stopped and you walked across the road." (This praise clearly teaches Adnan to commence walking after a car has stopped, and will increase his confidence to eventually initiate pedestrian crossing.) Once Adnan reached the island I pointed in the direction he now had to look. As soon as a car stopped, I repeated the road crossing technique.

The second, narrow crossing was impeded by tree branches and shrubs so it was important to position Adnan where he could be clearly visible to vehicle drivers. The safest and most visible position was about two steps onto the crossing. In this position Adnan could see traffic clearly and drivers could easily see him, especially when he wore a safety-colored item of clothing. On this crossing with less frequent traffic I said, "When there are no cars, or when the cars have stopped, you can walk." As there were no cars I simply said, "No cars—you can walk," and gently nudged him to walk across the crossing while praising him immediately after he took his first step. Over time, Adnan would learn to cross pedestrian crossings either when there were no vehicles or when the vehicles had stopped.

We walked the remainder of the route with Adnan observing the direction we were taking. He had a good memory for direction and we only needed to point out two landmarks (a red mailbox outside a house and a uniquely shaped tree) at two different locations to help him remember where he needed to turn. When we arrived at his workplace, we showed Adnan a quiet sheltered place where he could phone his aunt to confirm his arrival.

In the afternoon we met Adnan at work and walked the route back to Salma's home using the same landmarks and pedestrian crossings as before. Once Adnan arrived home we again praised him for the way he walked home. He then went into another room to enjoy some time by himself (secondary reinforcer).

5. Fading out and allowing the student to travel independently

Salma and Adnan continued the training to and from work twice a week. When Salma observed that Adnan was recognizing the correct time to cross at the pedestrian crossings she stood three steps to his side where he could see that she was not as close to him. She gave him the same instruction, "You go when the cars have stopped," and allowed him to initiate crossing the road. When he began to initiate the crossing she gave him immense praise, which motivated him to continue crossing without the need for her to physically prompt him. After a number of weeks of standing a few steps away from Adnan, Salma stood a meter or two behind him and gradually reduced her amount of praise.

When Salma believed Adnan was confident to cross the pedestrian crossings and had made no errors of judgment over a number of weeks, she set an initial performance criterion of ten times. That is:

- Adnan crossed at both pedestrian crossings consecutively, ten times, without prompts (with Salma observing him from 3 meters away).

- Then, Adnan crossed at both pedestrian crossings consecutively, six times, without prompts (with Salma observing him from another 5 meters away).

If Adnan had made any error of judgment during this time, then she would have retrained him until he was making no errors at all. She would repeat setting a criterion and moving away until she was satisfied that Adnan could cross both pedestrian crossings safely and confidently without error.

Once Adnan was crossing the pedestrian crossings independently, Salma gradually faded out from the rest of the route:

- First Adnan walked from home, crossed at both pedestrian crossings toward work consecutively, five times, without prompts (with Salma observing him from approximately 30 meters (100 feet) behind him). After the pedestrian crossings Adnan walked the rest of the way to work by himself.

- Second, Adnan walked from home, crossed at both pedestrian crossings to work consecutively five times without error (with Salma observing him from a distance away where he could not see her).

- Finally, Adnan simply left home and walked the entire route to work. Each time, he confirmed his arrival at work with a phone call.

- This entire process of fading out was repeated for the return route back home.

After Adnan had completed the forward and return routes, I recommended that he travel this route regularly over a number of months before introducing more complex skills like traveling on public transport. This would make the learning more concrete and increase his confidence without having to deal with additional travel experiences that might overwhelm him. This route was an important prerequisite to learning how to travel on public transport, as it allowed Adnan to learn to cope with longer routes which included negotiating a larger number of people, rain, and the idea of being further away from home.

CASE STUDY 6:   DAVID (32 YEARS)

Previous skills: Traveled three beginner routes independently and two intermediate routes that included traffic lights and pedestrian crossings

Route learned: Walk from work to the local football oval

Skills learned: Crossing at uncontrolled crossings

David lived in a group home with three other residents. Three days a week he walked to his supported workplace where he was employed as a process worker. David's workplace had recently formed a football team that played in a local competition. David was keen on sport and joined the team. He attended football training once a week after work, and was expected to walk to the football oval from work. The oval was not far from his workplace although the journey involved crossing two uncontrolled roads—a type of crossing David had never attempted independently. Uncontrolled roads are often the most complex of road crossing types because cars are not legally required to stop for pedestrians. Instead, pedestrians must judge the traffic flow and decide to cross at an appropriately safe time. Because of their complexity, uncontrolled crossings are usually the last type of crossing taught to students.

1. Understanding "Who is David?"

David had an intellectual disability, and was a confident person who enjoyed socializing. He was very helpful in the workplace and enjoyed answering the reception telephone during his lunch break. He had many interests, such as sport and cooking, and enjoyed using recipe books when it was his turn to make dinner at home.

David was highly motivated to learn the route to football training and—on his own—had arranged for a friend's mother to drive him home after training. Often, it was dark after training and David did not enjoy walking home at night. He had decided that, even if his friend's mother could not drive him home one night, he would call a taxi. Because David was familiar with independent travel and being safe on the roads he usually wore a brightly colored shirt (mainly red or yellow).

2. Establishing the travel-training goal

David had developed excellent travel skills such as seeking assistance if needed, using a mobile phone, crossing a variety of controlled road types, and interacting confidently in shops with members of the public. He enjoyed learning new travel routes but only if they had a purpose that was relevant to his interests.

Although other work colleagues walked to football training, there were times when David might have needed to walk to training alone (e.g. other colleagues might not have left work at the same time as him, or his friend who sometimes walked with him could be ill). (It's always important to teach students to travel alone, just in case they actually need to travel alone at some point and depend on their own skills instead of the skills of others.)

3. Planning the route prior to teaching

David worked in a supported environment where additional resources were available to assist employees. In David's workplace the staff trainers were keen to teach him the route from work to football training. Because travel-training requires a consistent and methodical teaching approach, we agreed that a maximum of two trainers teach David the route. Having any more trainers involved ran the risk of too many teaching variances that could affect the success of training. But the advantage of having two trainers was that if one was ill or on holiday, the other could continue to train David.

The two trainers accompanied me to review and plan the safest route to the football oval. We walked the route at the same time David would walk it and observed that it was afternoon peak traffic time. We noticed that one uncontrolled crossing was on a wider road on a hill without speed humps, so cars often exceeded the speed limit. If you stood toward either end of the road, then vehicles only came into view once they had reached the top of the hill. To make this crossing as safe as possible, David would need to cross the road at the top of the hill where he would have a full view of cars coming from both directions. Also, cars would be traveling at a slower speed as they ascended the hill. To help David remember the safest place to cross we decided we would use a green fence with a white letterbox near the crossing as a landmark.

The other uncontrolled road crossing was on a narrow road where cars were regularly parked in the afternoons. There was also a blind corner where drivers could not see the whole road until they had driven around the corner. To make this crossing safer, David would need to cross the road some distance away from the corner so that cars turning into it had plenty of time to see him. Also, he would need to step onto the road and position himself at the front of the first parked car so that drivers could see him clearly. To remind David where to cross the road we chose a unique-looking pole with a bright red sign on it as a landmark. We would teach David to cross the road in front of this sign.

The route was a short one that would take David about 15 minutes to walk and, given his extensive independent travel experience and strong motivation, we decided to train him using forward chaining. We divided the route into two segments:

1. from work to the other side of the first uncontrolled crossing

2. from the first uncontrolled crossing to the football oval (including the second uncontrolled crossing).

4. Training techniques used to teach the route

The two trainers, David, and I walked the route to the football oval. David walked confidently about ten steps ahead of us. When we arrived at the wide uncontrolled crossing on the hill, we walked to the white letterbox on the green fence. I explained to David that he would cross the road in front of this landmark because it was a safe place to cross. Once at the road edge I suggested to David that he cross the road when he thought it was safe. I was standing behind David, close enough to gently block him from crossing should he make an incorrect decision. It was important to invite David to cross the road first (instead of immediately teaching him how to cross) to help us determine his current skill level in deciding when to make an uncontrolled road crossing. David had traveled extensively over a number of years and had probably observed others crossing uncontrolled roads and perhaps already knew how to cross. (There is no point teaching a skill from the beginning if the student already has some level of knowledge and skill. Instead, teach what the student does not know.)

We observed David looking in both directions on the road but he seemed hesitant to cross, even when there was a reasonable amount of distance between him and a vehicle driving toward the hill. David was familiar with crossing at pedestrian crossings, where he crossed when either the cars had stopped or there were no cars at all. However, in this situation the road crossing rules were different, and David could cross if a car was a safe distance away. To help David determine when it was safe to cross we used two landmarks: in the right-hand direction, a large white building at a safe distance away, and in the left-hand direction, a large metal tower some distance away. I explained to David that if a car was driving before or near the white building and/or the metal tower then it was safe to cross the road. We then observed cars driving toward the white building and/or the metal tower: "David, the cars are near the white building/metal tower—it's safe to cross the road." I then gently nudged his back so that he took a step and I immediately praised him: "Well done David, the cars were… and it's safe to cross the road." Repeating this process over time increased David's confidence so that he was able to initiate this road crossing independently.

When we reached the narrow uncontrolled crossing we walked to the pole with the red sign. Again, I explained to David that this was the safe place to cross the road. We then walked to the road edge and onto the road next to the front of the parked car. I explained that he was to stand next to the parked car in front of the pole on this crossing. Again I invited David to cross the road. This road was quieter, with very few cars traveling on it. Standing behind David I observed that he looked many times in both directions. An infrequent car drove past. He continued to stand at the edge, though he leant forward when there were no cars. He appeared to be trying to gather his courage to make the decision to cross. It seemed he was making a correct judgment when to cross the road. I said to David to encourage him to cross, "Good David—you cross when you think it's safe." He stood there a little longer and when there were no cars he took one step forward. Immediately I praised him: "Well done David—there are no cars and you are crossing the road." He quickened his pace with confidence, having received confirmation that his decision and action were correct. Importantly, praise was only given *after* he had initiated the first step across the road. In this way, David did not become dependent on the trainer to imply or tell him when to cross the road, which enabled the trainer to fade out from the program.

Having crossed the road, the football oval was within a short walking distance. David walked the remainder of the route independently. Once at the oval, he rang the trainer to confirm his arrival.

5. Fading out and allowing the student to travel independently

Once the trainer observed that David was consistently making correct road crossing decisions, a performance criterion was set. Following the rule that the more complex and dangerous a travel situation the higher the criterion, the trainer set an initial criterion of ten observations on both crossings standing back about 1 meter (3 feet) from David. Once David had achieved crossing both roads safely and consecutively ten times, the trainer observed him another eight times at about 2 meters (6 feet) away. Again, once achieved, the trainer moved about 5 meters (16 feet) away and observed him another eight times. The trainer repeated this process until she was a great distance from David at both road crossings.

Once the trainers had completed fading out from the riskier road crossings, they commenced fading out from the entire route in the following way:

1. They walked at a great distance behind David to the second red pole crossing and observed him cross safely, from a distance, five times.

2. Once David had successfully walked five times to the red pole, the trainers observed him walk from work to the first crossing near the hill, five times.

3. Once David had achieved this, the trainers were satisfied that he could walk the route safely and independently.

David had now learned to cross at two complex, uncontrolled road crossings. However, more importantly, he had learned to trust his own judgment, which increased his travel skill level and confidence. If David wished, he now had a solid skill set on which to learn how to travel on public transport.

Routes for advanced travelers

CASE STUDY 7:   TANYA (17 YEARS)

Previous skills: Traveled block routes, a range of crossing types, and traveled independently on four routes in her local area

Route learned: From school to college

Skills learned: Traveling on a bus

Tanya had commenced travel-training at ten years of age. In the last seven years she had learned to walk four routes that included block routes, traffic lights, pedestrian crossings, and uncontrolled crossings, and she enjoyed buying items in the local shop for her family. She had also learned to phone her mother when she arrived at her destination. Tanya was in her final year at high school and as part of the curriculum she was expected to travel from school to college once a week to attend a "life skills" course. Her school was about a block away from the bus stop from where she could catch a bus to college. It would take Tanya about 45 minutes to travel the entire route.

1. Understanding "Who is Tanya?"

Tanya had Down syndrome and frequently experienced asthma. She enjoyed traveling independently and her confidence increased with each new route she learned. As her travel-training skills progressed, she became increasingly familiar with various training approaches and, as a result, learned new skills and routes quickly. Tanya was sociable, had many friends, and enjoyed talking with people. She knew she shouldn't initiate conversations with strangers, although because this desire was very strong, her mother, Helen, allowed her to initiate conversation with "mothers with a pram." Although it is only an assumption that "mothers with prams" are safe people, it has proved to be a reasonable one and Helen was prepared to take this risk. If Tanya was not given some leeway to talk when in public, then it appeared she did so anyway with any person walking along the street.

Tanya developed a fear of dogs early in life because a neighbour's dog had chased her. In her first travel-training program she had learned the "avoid dog" strategy, although she still liked to watch a video of herself performing this action (video self-modeling). Watching the video reminded and comforted her that she could successfully perform this technique when approached by a dog. Sometimes at home, she would practice the action with her mother.

Tanya's asthma left her short of breath when walking longer distances. When this happened, she would inhale medication and rest for about ten minutes before continuing. Whenever she walked a route by herself, she would take a bright red backpack, which had been encouraged in her initial travel-training program. Sometimes she also wore a bright shirt.

2. Setting the travel-training goal

Tanya's school required her to learn the route to college. After college, Helen would meet her and drive her home or back to school. Once Tanya could catch a bus from school to college—and had consolidated this skill over three or four months—we could start to train the reverse journey, but this would happen at a later date. Learning one route at a time would allow her to increase her confidence on the route so that it became routine and easy to travel. Given Tanya's solid foundation skills and extensive independent travel, she was ready to learn how to catch the bus. She was highly motivated to learn the route as she was looking forward to attending the college and meeting her friends there.

3. Planning the route prior to teaching

A teacher's aide at the school agreed to teach Tanya the route to college. Together, we traveled the route to investigate exactly what it involved. The five-minute walk from school to the bus stop included one uncontrolled crossing. There was a blue mailbox which we could use as a landmark situated in a safe place where Tanya could cross the road. At the bus stop there was no shelter, which meant Tanya would need to take a raincoat to protect her from rain. Although there was a seat nearby, we would teach Tanya to stand near the bus stop so that she could wave the bus down as it approached. We noticed a drain cover beside the bus stop that could be used as a landmark upon which she could stand. The drain cover was positioned a safe distance from the curb so that she would not be hit by a bus, but close enough so that the bus driver could see her and stop.

Previously, we had checked the bus timetable and noticed there were two buses driving to the college. We decided to teach Tanya to catch just one of these buses so as to not confuse her. Tanya was good at matching so we decided she would carry a cue card in her wallet with the bus number 744 written on it. When she arrived at the stop, she could take out the card and match it to the bus with the same number.

The aide and I boarded the 744 bus. We noticed the location of the bus ticket system (a tap on/tap off system), as well as a brightly painted car repair business that Tanya could use as a landmark to prompt her to ring the bell so that she could exit the bus at the correct location. Once we left the bus we walked about a kilometer (half a mile) to the traffic lights opposite the college. Along this walk were various seats where Tanya could rest if she wished.

Tanya's classroom was on level 2 of the building in room 203, and it was an easy walk upstairs to find her room. She also had the option of taking the lift, and we included this skill in her training. We noticed there were toilets close to her classroom, as well as a café should she want to buy items. We would train Tanya how to use these facilities.

Because the route was lengthy, despite Tanya's ability to travel independently, we broke it into two segments to make it easier to learn:

1. from school to the exit bus stop near the college

2. from the exit bus stop to the college classroom.

We decided to backward chain the route (i.e. teach segment 2 first) because the aide had a limited amount of time in the morning to teach Tanya. This way, Tanya could become independent on segment 2 fairly quickly (walking from the exit bus stop to her classroom) and maintain her motivation and her confidence, and the aide would initially drive her to the exit bus stop. Once she was independent in segment 2, the aide would start to train segment 1 (from school to the exit bus stop), leaving her able to make her way to her college independently.

4. Training techniques used to teach the route

On the morning of the first training session, Tanya and her mother viewed the brief video of Tanya applying the "avoid dog" strategy. Watching this video reminded Tanya of what she needed to do when approached by a dog and gave her confidence that she could do this when required. We recommended that she watch the video each morning she was to travel to college and as often as she wanted to.

During the first training session the aide and I accompanied Tanya and we drove from her school to the exit bus stop. Once we had arrived at the exit stop we explained we were about to walk to her college classroom. We also explained that if she needed to stop and take her asthma medication, then that was fine, and that there were many seats along the route if she wanted to rest. During the walk there was a fork on the path, where we could turn left or right. So that she would not forget to turn right we pointed out that on the right side there was a cake shop with lots of cakes displayed in the window. Having a sweet tooth, Tanya took notice of this landmark.

To reinforce using the seats along the route, and noticing she was becoming short of breath, we invited her to sit down. She took out her medication and used it, which we reinforced as a great idea ("Well done, Tanya—you used your medication when you felt breathless"). A few minutes later she was ready to walk the remainder of the route. She crossed at the traffic lights independently and we showed her to the classroom. We also showed her where to find the toilets but did not introduce the lift or the café, as this would have been too much information to absorb at this early training stage.

Instead, we taught her these additional locations once Tanya demonstrated in the following weeks that she knew her way to college and appeared reasonably confident. We reinforced to Tanya that because we had arrived at college she could phone her mother outside the classroom in a quiet place near a window. She agreed and phoned Helen who gave her lots of praise for reaching her destination. Tanya was very pleased and took note of the window where she would ring the following week.

After about four weeks (four sessions) of walking this route, Tanya began to walk a few meters ahead of us from the exit bus stop, obviously knowing the route to her classroom, and rang her mother on arrival. On one occasion during this time she also sat down for a brief rest. We believed she had the skills to walk this section of the route independently, though to test this we needed to set a performance criterion.

5. Fading out and allowing the student to travel independently

This segment of the route was low risk as it only involved one traffic light crossing, so we set an initial observation criterion of eight times. That is, from about 6 meters (20 feet) the aide observed Tanya traveling the route on eight occasions with no prompting. Once this had been accomplished, the aide set another observation criterion of five times from approximately 12 meters (40 feet) behind Tanya. Following the success of this criterion, the aide agreed to meet Tanya at her destination three times; at the exit bus stop the aide informed Tanya that she would not see her on the route but would meet her outside her room once she had phoned her mother. The aide then said goodbye and, without being seen by Tanya, walked on the opposite side of the road at some distance behind her. The aide also used a monocular to help her observe Tanya. Once this criterion was achieved, the aide had observed Tanya walking segment 2 (from the exit bus stop to her classroom) 16 times without assistance, which was more than adequate to conclude she could now walk this section of the route safely and independently.

From school to the bus stop

The next step in the travel-training program was to teach segment 1 of the route (walking from school to the bus stop and taking the bus to the exit stop). Of course, once at the exit bus stop Tanya would walk the remainder of the route to college independently as she had now learned this section of the route. The main strategies used for teaching segment 1 were repetitive training and positive reinforcement. Sometimes, especially if the student is learning to use a bus for the first time or appears nervous, it is helpful to drive the route first in a car, before catching the bus. This helps the student become familiar with the bus route and often helps to reduce their nervousness.

The major teaching points on this section were for Tanya to stand in the correct position on the drain cover at the bus stop; flag down the correct bus after using her matching cue card to confirm the correct bus number (744); board the bus and use the tap on/tap off ticket system; locate a seat close to the driver; ring the bell at the car repair business; then exit the bus. There was a lot to teach and learn in this route segment, and a description of how to teach the more difficult aspects follows.

- Tanya was confident crossing uncontrolled roads, having crossed a variety of these road types as an intermediate traveler. Therefore, the only aspect we needed to teach her was the landmark (a blue mailbox) situated away from the road corner that would indicate the safe place at which to cross this road.

- Once Tanya was standing on the drain cover next to the bus stop she took out her cue card with 744 written in bold black lettering. As each bus arrived the trainer pointed to the number on the bus and asked Tanya, "Is this the same as the number on your card?" Because Tanya was skilled at matching she quickly learned to identify the correct bus using her cue card. (However, if this had been difficult for her, then we would have practiced "matching training" at home before commencing this part of the route. For example, her mother might have videoed buses pulling up at her bus stop and they could practice matching these with her cue card at home. An alternative method is to have two or three bus numbers in front of Tanya, and have her match the correct number by comparing them to her cue card. The point is to think about the strengths of your student and use their strengths to solve problems. For students who find matching difficult, a trainer might teach them to board each bus and ask the driver if this bus is the 744, or hand the driver a card asking if theirs was the right bus.)

- Seating position in the bus was very important. Tanya was encouraged to sit as close to the driver as possible. This prevented her from being lost in a crowded bus and possibly missing her bus stop, as well as being able to talk to the driver if she needed assistance. Also, Tanya was taught how to hold on safely while standing up when no seats were available.

- Before teaching her bus travel, we drove the bus route with Tanya to familiarize her to the landmark (a car repair business) where she would ring the bus bell to exit the bus. While traveling in the bus we reminded Tanya to keep a lookout for the car repair business. As soon as the bus was near the repair business, Tanya was prompted to ring the bell and was praised for doing so.

When Tanya began to initiate behaviors such as identifying the correct bus, waving it down, sitting in the correct position, and ringing the bus bell, it was time to commence the fading process.

On the bus, the trainer sat closely behind Tanya. The performance criterion was for Tanya to ring the bus bell at the landmark (the car repair business) consecutively and independently five times. Once she achieved this, the aide sat further away from Tanya and set a criterion of three times before moving back further. The goal was to continue moving away gradually once the criterion had been achieved until the aide was seated at the back of the bus, as far away as possible from Tanya. Once Tanya achieved the final criterion in the bus, she had succeeded in ringing the bus bell 100 percent of the time over many months.

The next step was that Tanya traveled on the bus by herself while the aide met her at the exit bus stop. A five-time criterion was set and Tanya successfully completed this. She was then deemed independent on this entire route from school to college.

Importantly, before introducing additional public transport routes, Tanya was allowed to travel the route for some months. This helped increase her travel experience and confidence—a prerequisite for more complex public transport travel routes.

CASE STUDY 8:   PAUL (18 YEARS)

Previous skills: Had learned block routes, a range of crossing types, independent travel on buses across the city

Route learned: From home to school

Skills learned: Traveling on a train

Paul's school bus had recently changed its route, adding an extra 20 minutes to an already lengthy trip. Paul and his parents agreed that taking the train to school would be a quicker and a more efficient travel option.

1. Understanding "Who is Paul?"

Paul had autism and an intellectual disability. He was a confident traveler who avoided talking to people in public as often as he could. He had some good strategies for avoiding conversation. He always wore dark sunglasses and a red peaked cap positioned so that the peak touched the top of his sunglasses. He traveled wearing a pair of over-the-ear headphones: sometimes he listened to music but mostly the earphones were worn to block out excessive noise and to avoid conversation with other people. These appeared to be effective strategies as others rarely interrupted him. Paul preferred to travel outside peak hours and would travel on the school bus very early in the morning to avoid other school students, especially those who traveled in groups. He would also find and use "safe areas" (e.g. a quiet corner on a road; under a tree away from the crowds) where he would wait until excessive crowds left the area.

2. Establishing the travel-training goal

Paul was familiar with the ten-minute walk from his home to the train station. His father, Stan, caught the train to and from work daily and Paul would often walk to the station to meet his father on an evening, and they would walk home together.

We decided that Stan would teach Paul the route to school, beginning early in the morning so that Paul could avoid excessive crowds and Stan could arrive at work on time. Because Paul already knew the route to the station, Stan left home ten minutes before Paul and they met each other at the station near the train destination board. The travel-training goal for Paul would be to travel on the train from the station, exit the train near his school, and walk the short route to school.

3. Planning the route prior to teaching

Stan and I met at the train station early one morning at the same time he would travel the route with Paul. We traveled the route together to investigate what was involved in teaching it to Paul.

At the station were three train platforms with trains traveling in different directions. The destination board indicated that Paul's platform was number 2. We proceeded to platform 2 and noticed there was another destination board positioned high above the heads of travelers. Importantly, this board was located where the train's driver compartment would be situated—a safe location to board the train. It was essential that Paul stood within reading distance of the board so that he could check whether any given train traveled to his train stop. We chose a drink machine to serve as a landmark where Paul could wait on the platform and read the destination board.

When the train arrived, we boarded the carriage next to the driver's compartment—a safe place to travel as help can be sought quickly from the driver if needed. Stan and I noted that there were six stops on the route to Paul's school. Stan mentioned that Paul used a mobile phone app when traveling on the bus to alert him when he was coming to his stop. Stan suggested that Paul could use a similar app on the train to alert him when he was coming into his station. Although Paul could easily read the station names as he passed through, this app was comforting and gave him confidence that he would not miss his stop.

When we exited the train we walked the short route to Paul's school. On this route there were two pedestrian crossings. Both crossings experienced little traffic at that time in the morning and would not be difficult for Paul to cross, given his extensive road crossing experience. There were several quiet locations along the route where Paul could retreat—although given the few pedestrians at that time in the morning he would probably not need them.

Because Paul was an experienced, motivated, and capable traveler we reduced the route into only two segments:

1. from the home train station to the exit train station

2. from the exit train station to school.

The walking route from the exit train station to school was short and Paul would remember it once shown, so we decided to forward chain the route. That is, we would first teach him how to take the train (segment 1), and then walk with him to school (segment 2). As a back-up strategy, toward the end of the training program, even though Paul had his phone app we would still orient him to about three train stations beyond his destination and teach him how to return to his destination just in case he ever missed his stop. Also, in future, if Paul learned other train routes, he would be able to generalize this important back-up strategy.

4. Training techniques used to teach the route

During the first training session with Paul, Stan and I pointed out the learning points on the route. We showed Paul the destination board, where we gave him time to locate the name of the exit stop. Paul used a cue card with the stop name written on it so he could match the card with the destination board. We showed Paul the platform number that appeared next to his stop on the destination board. (Always teach a student to check the destination board for their platform number, and never assume that the platform number will stay the same, even if there are only two platforms going in opposite directions. I have experienced a number of occasions where platforms have been changed due to a breakdown or other incidents on the tracks.)

We walked to platform 2, which Paul had confirmed by checking the platform number. We pointed out the drink machine landmark, stood beside it, and Paul checked the destination board again to confirm the train arriving at the platform went to his destination. As we boarded, we reinforced that this was the compartment next to the driver's and explained that, if another person ever confronted him, he could contact the driver by knocking on the door or pressing a red button that was located in this carriage.

Days before this training session Stan and Paul had practiced using the mobile phone app, which alerted Paul of his station exit stop. Once on the train Paul used this app efficiently to locate his stop. Along the way we also asked him to read the station signs on each platform to confirm he knew their location so that he could also check visually if he wished to. As we were nearing the exit stop we encouraged Paul to prepare to exit by standing near the door. Once off the train, we provided Paul with praise and reviewed the positive behaviors he had performed on this section of the route.

We then encouraged Paul to walk a few meters ahead of us so that he could observe the route without distraction. When needed, we prompted him to go right or left at a certain point. Paul crossed both pedestrian crossings without error and when we were in viewing distance of the school he walked the remainder of the route by himself. On his arrival, he rang his mother to confirm his arrival.

Through repetitive training and positive reinforcement, Paul was confidently traveling this route without any prompts in two weeks (ten sessions). At this stage, Stan and Paul implemented the back-up strategy of traveling to the next three stations, just in case Paul ever missed his stop. At each station Stan explained how to return to his exit station should he accidently travel beyond it, and Paul was required to demonstrate that he could apply this procedure at each station. Once the back-up strategy had been taught, Stan believed Paul could travel this route by himself and began the fading-out procedure of setting criteria.

5. Fading out and allowing the student to travel independently

To commence fading out from this route Stan set an initial criterion of five times. That is:

- Stan observed Paul on the train consecutively five times, without prompts, from the back of the driver's compartment.

- Stan observed Paul consecutively five times walking to school from 10 meters (32 feet) behind.

Once Paul had achieved this criterion, Stan set another criterion of five times, watching from further away.

- Stan observed Paul on the train consecutively five times, without prompts, from the window of the next train compartment.

- Stan observed Paul consecutively five times walking to school from 20 meters (65 feet) behind on the other side of the road.

Once achieved, Stan set a three-times criterion.

- Stan observed Paul on the train consecutively three times, without prompts, from a place in the train where Paul could not see Stan.

- Stan observed Paul walking to school three times consecutively from the other side of the road at a greater distance.

When Paul achieved this, Stan drove to the exit train station, allowing Paul to travel on the train by himself. He set a criterion of three times.

- Stan observed Paul three times walking to school from the exit station platform, following Paul without him realizing it.

This final criterion was necessary because Paul's behavior or confidence might possibly change when alone. During this final three-times criterion, Stan saw a person approach Paul asking for the time, as well as a group of students walking the same route to school. In both of these situations, Paul appeared to react appropriately and remained calm and focused. After Paul had satisfied the three-times criterion, he traveled the route independently without being observed. Overall, Stan faded out from the training program over 16 sessions. It is unlikely, given this gradual process, that Paul would have difficulty traveling this route.

CASE STUDY 9:   RITA (43 YEARS)

Previous skills: An experienced traveler on buses and trains

Route learned: From home to the city to meet friends

Skills learned: A new bus and train route into the city

Rita lived independently with a friend in an apartment close to her parent's home. She received her first travel-training program at 14 years and had developed excellent travel skills enabling her to travel independently to work and to a range of leisure activities using buses and trains. She has been able to generalize her travel-training skills to new routes (reading bus numbers and train destination boards, implementing back-up strategies such as asking for directions) although on rare occasions she still required formal training to learn complex routes.

Recently, her social group decided to meet monthly in a café in the central business district (CBD) in her city. From the café they would move on to various activities around the city. Rita believed she needed assistance to navigate the complex bus and train system into the CBD and be shown the safest route to walk to the café. Although Rita was an advanced traveler, each step of travel-training must be followed diligently for the training program to be completed successfully.

1. Understanding "Who is Rita?"

Rita was a social, confident, and motivated person who valued her independence. She worked at the local post office packing items and sorting mail, and spent evenings with friends enjoying a range of leisure activities. Rita had an intellectual disability and if she didn't understand what people were telling her she would ask for clarification. She was observant, had a good memory, and learned quickly through repetition. Because she had traveled independently for years she was confident using a mobile phone, and familiar with the requirements of traveling on public transport and using landmarks.

2. Establishing the travel-training goal

Rita defined the travel-training goal herself—traveling from home to the CBD café to meet her friends and learning how get back home again. She asked her mother, Alice, to help her become familiar with these routes. Although Alice had taught Rita many routes over the years, because of the complexity of this one, she sought my assistance to ensure the components of the route were the safest and most direct.

3. Planning the route prior to teaching

Alice and I met to review the route—a lengthy one that would take Rita about 90 minutes to travel one way. We decided that she would learn the forward route from home first, travel that route for a month or two, and then learn the return route back home. In the interim, she would return home by taxi. The route involved:

1. walking from home to the bus depot

2. traveling on a bus to the train station

3. train travel to the CBD (Sussex train station)

4. walking 15 minutes from Sussex train station to the café.

Rita already knew how to walk to the bus depot as she had caught buses from the depot over several years. Many buses drove to or past the train station, although they went at irregular times. Rita needed to meet her friends at the café each Saturday at 10a.m. The train station was large with 12 platforms. There were seven platforms with trains going to the CBD, so we needed a strategy to help Rita know which platform to wait on for the next CBD train. Once in the CBD, it was a 15-minute walk to the café through dense traffic and crowded streets. The walk involved four ATS traffic light crossings. There were shortcuts up two alleyways from the train station to the café, but we decided not to include them in the route as they were narrow, gloomy, and potentially dangerous.

We decided to forward chain the route because Rita had extensive travel skills and only needed to learn basic elements such as bus and train identification strategies and platform numbers.

4. Training techniques used to teach the route

Because Rita already knew the route from her home to the bus depot we agreed to meet her there early on Saturday morning. Alice and I had done our research and knew Rita could travel on one of three buses to the train station (bus numbers 660, 661, 664). Alice had created a cue card with these numbers written down. Given Rita's bus travel experience, she was easily able to identify the buses using her cue card. We boarded a bus to the train station—a route familiar to Rita. Rita rang the bus bell and exited at the train station, without prompting or assistance. She walked to the train destination board and recognized that several trains traveled to the CBD. However, she was confused and needed help to identify which platform had the next departing city-bound train. Therefore, as a reliable measure we suggested to Rita that she approach a ticket box to ask the railway attendant which platform to go to for the train to Sussex station in about 20 minutes. (We judged that 20 minutes would allow her enough time to walk to the platform, position herself, and wait for the train without having to rush.) The attendant suggested platform 4 and we walked to this platform.

Once on the train, Rita read each station name along the way until she reached Sussex station. We exited the train and walked the route to the café. We noticed Rita was confident crossing the roads and she also noted landmarks to remind her where she needed to go, for example, turn right at the cinema and left at the computer shop. We arrived at the café close to 10a.m.

and some of her friends had already arrived. Being familiar with the process of catching a taxi, Alice only needed to show her the taxi rank next to the café where she could take a taxi home later in the day.

5. Fading out and allowing the student to travel independently

Rita and Alice traveled the route every Saturday morning for three weeks. At the end of the third week Alice could stand back and Rita negotiated this route without assistance. Alice knew it was time to fade out, and set an initial observation criterion of five times. Alice observed Rita at a distance from the bus stop and from the middle of the bus, as well as walking to the café about 20 meters behind. (These seem to be large distances from which to observe in the first instance; however, this is appropriate given Rita's extensive travel experience and capability.) Once Rita had traveled the route with Alice at a distance, Alice observed her another five times from the back of the bus, then at a distance to the café where she could not be seen by Rita. Once this criterion had been achieved, Alice set an eight-times criterion where she would observe Alice from the train station to the café at a distance where she could not be seen.

Once this final criterion had been achieved, Rita traveled the route every Saturday by herself. Overall, Alice had observed Rita traveling independently over 18 Saturdays. (This might appear excessive for an individual with such capability as Rita, but to minimize risk, a gradual fading-out process is essential.)

Top Tips for Trainers

I have mentioned these "top tips" in various chapters of the book, and they come to life in the case studies in Chapter 10, which I highly recommend you read. But the ideas here are so important that it's worth summarizing them in a page or two, for easy reference.

- When travel-training, always choose a route that is relevant to, and rewarding for, your student, and is genuinely a part of their life.

- Structure the journey and the landmarks and keep them consistent. But be flexible about the level of assistance you provide, and about the amount and timing of positive feedback (reinforcement).

- Use the minimum amount of prompting possible that still results in your student performing each step successfully. The more they can do without your help the better (after all, that is the goal). Also, it's much easier to fade out from a training situation if they are not relying on cues from you.

- Don't talk to your student during training other than to teach a skill or to praise them for doing a particular step correctly. When they get a step correct, reinforce them immediately afterwards, and be specific about what they have done well.

- Teach your student in the real situation (out in the world), but start with less complicated (less risky) routes and build up from there. Once they have mastered a route, give them time to consolidate their skills and build confidence before starting to train an additional, more complex route.

- Teach back-up strategies and extra skills to build in safety for your student. The particular strategies will depend on the student, their experience and capabilities, and the type of route you are teaching. Examples include the student phoning (say) their parent to tell them they have arrived; how and when to approach someone for help; stranger danger; and what to do if they travel past their stop.

- If more than one trainer is teaching a route, it's very important to stay coordinated and to teach consistently. Where possible, have no more than two trainers teach a student on a route.

- Always fade out slowly from training a student. Adhere to the particular performance criteria you have set, which will prove their level of independence. The riskier the situation for the student, the more gradually the trainer should fade out. Another benefit of fading out slowly is seeing how your student manages in unusual circumstances or if they become distracted, and being close by to step in and teach them coping strategies, if needed.

- Finally, improve your student's safety by making sure they are highly visible to drivers. Teach them the habit of wearing or carrying something (from the waist up) in bright red, bright yellow, or bright orange. Make wearing a safety color part of their routine for travel-training.

Teaching a person with a disability to travel independently is at the very core of individualized training. The route you choose, the landmarks, the cues and reinforcers, and the back-up strategies simply *must* be tailored to each learner. While training is often very structured, trainers also need the skills—and attitude—to think creatively, be positive and flexible, and to problem solve.

Glossary

Audio-tactile signal (ATS) Push-button systems at traffic lights which give pedestrians signals to show when to and when not to cross the road. Traffic lights are fitted with audio-tactile devices which can be easily heard, felt, and seen by pedestrians with a variety of disabilities.

Augmentative and alternative communication (AAC) devices A broad term that includes communication methods that replace or enhance a person's speech or writing. AAC is used by people who have difficulty with speech or language. An example of an AAC device is an iPhone with an AAC app with voice output.

Autism A lifelong neurodevelopmental condition characterized by the way an individual relates to their environment and interacts with other people. The word "spectrum" describes the range of challenges that people with autism might experience and the degree to which they might be affected. The main areas that are affected include social communication, social interaction, and restricted or repetitive behaviors and interests. People on the autism spectrum might also have sensory sensitivities such as avoiding everyday sounds and textures like vacuum cleaners, particular songs, hairdryers, or sand. They might also have an intellectual impairment or learning difficulty. An estimated one in 100 people has autism, which affects almost four times as many boys than girls.

Back-up strategy Used by students to reduce risks when traveling. These strategies are taught during the travel-training program so the student can use them if they experience difficulty while traveling. Examples are using a mobile phone to seek assistance, or using earphones to block out disturbing noise.

Backward chaining Breaking down a task, such as a travel route, into small steps, and then teaching the steps one at a time in reverse order (Z, Y, then X). Teaching the last step (Z) first provides the student with an immediate understanding about the purpose of the task (e.g. arriving at the shop to buy an item), which helps keep motivation high. Chaining, that is, breaking down the route, also reduces training time in that you do not need to teach the whole route at one time, which is very time-consuming and possibly tiring for the student and trainer.

Block route A route in the shape of a block with four corners. The pathways join at each corner and there are no road crosses.

Cognitive behavior therapy (CBT) A form of treatment that assists individuals in changing unhelpful or unhealthy thinking habits, feelings, and behaviors. Once unhelpful thinking and behavioral patterns are recognized the individual can consciously replace these patterns with new ones that reduce anxiety and enhance coping skills. CBT has been used successfully to treat anxiety, depression, low self-esteem, uncontrollable anger, substance abuse, and eating disorders.

Continuous reinforcement Reinforcing a particular behavior each time it occurs (e.g. continuous praise). The goal is for that behavior to keep reoccurring. This is used when teaching a new skill and signals to the student that this behavior should continue as it is a desirable behavior. Once the student engages in the desired behavior the trainer usually progresses to partial reinforcement to ensure the behavior continues.

Controlled crossing A road crossing on a main road or in a high-density traffic area with audio-tactile signals, traffic signals, or markers that control the flow of traffic.

Criteria setting Once a trainer believes that a student is competent at a skill, such as crossing a particular road, a performance criterion is set to check whether or not this is actually the case. The more complex or dangerous the skill the higher the criterion. For example, if a student is crossing an uncontrolled road, then the trainer will observe approximately 1 meter away from the student consecutively ten times. If the student successfully reaches the criterion and crosses the road successfully ten times, then the trainer moves further away and sets another criterion. This pattern continues until the teacher has faded out from the program. If the student makes an error, then the trainer reteaches the skill and resets the criterion and starts observing once again from the first observation.

Cue card A durable card with words written on it to help a student communicate a message or to remember information. Examples include a card shown to a bus driver which says, "Can you please stop at the Berkeley Street bus stop," or a card with a bus number on it to remind the student which bus to board.

Down syndrome A chromosome disorder in which people are born with 47 chromosomes in the cells instead of 46. It affects one in every 700–900 babies. Traits of Down syndrome include specific physical features, some health and development challenges, and a level of intellectual disability.

Fading out The gradual withdrawal of prompts and the trainer's presence from the travel-training program to enable the student to travel independently.

Forward chaining Reducing a task, such as a travel route, into small steps and teaching them one at a time in forward order (A, B, then C). Once a student can perform A independently the trainer then has them perform A and teaches B. When B is mastered the student does A and B independently and learns C. Once C is learned the student has mastered the route.

Goal setting A travel-training intention with a specific beginning and end—for example, the student will walk from home to a specific shop to purchase an item of choice.

Independent travel A student traveling safely and confidently without assistance. The student can be traveling alone or accompanied (e.g. with a friend).

Intellectual disability A lifelong disability characterized by limitations in both intellectual functioning and adaptive behavior in everyday social and practical skills. IQ is assessed at 70 or under.

Landmark Any unique and permanent object in the environment that is easily seen by the student. A landmark can be used to help a student understand exactly where to cross a road or ring a bell to stop a bus, or determine at which point in the distance a car must be for it to be safe to cross the road (e.g. the car is near the yellow building so is far enough away to cross the road safely).

Learning impairment A learning impairment is unrelated to a person's intellectual capacity. Rather, a learning impairment is the result of a central nervous system dysfunction and can affect reading, writing, speaking, reasoning, and so on. Examples of learning impairment include dyslexia, dysgraphia (impairment in handwriting, organizing ideas, spelling), non-verbal learning disability (unable to coordinate abstract thought to practical implication), math difficulty, and an inability to organize.

Modeling prompts A demonstration of a skill or task by the trainer so that the student can learn by imitation.

Monocular An optical instrument used with one eye to magnify distant objects, resembling one half of a pair of binoculars. A monocular is small and lightweight. It can be used by the trainer from a distance to observe students during the process of fading out from a program.

Partial reinforcement Where some but not all correct responses or behaviors receive positive reinforcement (e.g. praise). Partial reinforcement tends to make the desired response stronger so the response continues over time—the student needs to "work harder" to get the praise. Trainers generally provide partial reinforcement to a student when they are performing a skill or task with limited (if any) assistance during the latter part of training. Once the student continues to perform a skill or task accurately, then partial reinforcement is faded out and the desired behavior should continue to occur. For example, when a student learns to ring the bus bell at a particular landmark and is beginning to consistently perform the skill, the trainer only provides reinforcement sometimes (perhaps the second ring, then the fifth ring, then the eighth ring).

Pedestrian crossing An area of the road painted in broad white stripes where vehicles must stop for pedestrians. A pedestrian crossing is a controlled crossing.

Physical prompt Where the trainer uses physical contact with the student to guide the learner through a skill or activity. For example, the trainer may request the student to push the bell button on a bus at a particular road crossing, and then physically prompt the student by guiding the student's hand to the bell and assist them to ring the bell.

Positive reinforcement Providing a reward such as praise ("Well done Lucy—there are no cars and you are walking across the road") *immediately after* a desired response (such as Lucy initiating walking across the road).

Roundabout A circular intersection where vehicles travel in a clockwise direction (in Australia) around a central island on the road. Drivers yield to cars on their right-hand side (again, in Australia) before entering the roundabout and then exit at their desired street. Avoid training students to cross at roundabouts.

Route planning Investigating the safest route, then considering the best way to teach that route to a specific student—for example, investigating the safest walking route from home to the local shop, deciding to teach the route in small segments, and defining these segments.

Route segmentation Reducing an entire travel route into small segments before teaching each segment in either a backward or forward chain. The size of the segment depends on the complexity of the route, and the student's ability to learn each segment. For example, an advanced traveler might need the route reduced into only two segments. However, a student undertaking their first route might need to reduce a less complex route into more segments so it is easier to learn.

Secondary reinforcer The value of secondary reinforcers is learned through experience. For example, when a student provides a correct response (e.g. rings the bus bell at a given landmark) the trainer might provide them with a dollar coin. They have learned that they can make a purchase with this coin and it becomes a motivator for them to continue ringing the bus bell.

Shaping (or behavior shaping) The student's behavior is shaped or molded by the trainer so that a desired response results. For example, the trainer may take the student's hand and together they push the bus bell so that the student learns the way to approach this skill.

Stranger danger The danger to children and adults presented by strangers or people unknown to them. In travel-training programs students are taught strategies to cope with strangers who might present a threat.

Tactile defensiveness A behavior and emotional response where individuals are sensitive to touch sensations. Having such negative tactile reactions often result in individuals feeling overwhelmed and fearful of ordinary daily activities. It also influences the type or amount of physical prompting a trainer can use to shape a learner's behavior.

Travel-training (or travel instruction) Intensive one-to-one instruction designed to teach sighted people who have disabilities how to travel safely and confidently on routes in the community.

Uncontrolled crossing A road crossing, usually on quieter roads with less traffic, without audio-tactile signals, traffic signals, or markers of any kind. Traffic flows freely without interference.

Verbal prompt Verbal assistance that helps students learn target skills correctly: for example, "Good. There are no cars—what do you need to do now?"

Video modeling Observational learning where a student watches a video of another individual demonstrating desired behaviors—for example, watching a video of an individual pushing the button at traffic lights and crossing the road correctly.

Video self-modeling Where individuals observe themselves correctly performing desired behaviors and then imitate the target behavior in real life. The video serves as a reminder about the way to correctly perform an action.

Visual cues A visual form of communication to assist learning, for example, pointing in the direction of a car which has stopped to allow the student to cross the road. Pointing to the car while saying, "The car has stopped—it is safe to walk," makes this point more powerful and can direct the student's attention directly to the car. Visual cues also include, for example, symbols printed on cardboard (e.g. a picture of a milk bottle that the student will purchase from a shop) or a "thumbs-up" signal by a trainer to indicate that the student has performed well.

Encouragement from Parents and Professionals

I have been very fortunate to work with many dedicated people over the years. Although these letters and comments reflect the parents' or professionals' appreciation for the travel-training service, much of the success is also attributed to their effort, hard work, and trust. These comments and endorsements (a snapshot only) were forwarded to me between 1990 and 2015. The names of people and places are pseudonyms.

I was given the task of travel-training a service user I case manage at our day center. I found this a daunting prospect without much guidance on how to go about this process. Thank goodness for Desirée! She came in, assessed the service user and provided a simple, stress-free strategy to travel-train him and work with the skills he already had. Her strategy focused on gradually allowing him to feel more and more independent rather than relying on staff prompting. He is well on his way to being able to travel independently, a victory for him and a great relief for his mother. I am so grateful for Desirée's support, her friendly and professional demeanour, and thorough travel-training strategies which will make a huge impact on the life and independence of this service user.

Kind regards, Keith

Written by an allied health case manager in 2015. His client was 22 at the time.

Dear Desirée,

The staff and students of Barton College would like to thank you for providing travel-training to students and staff. Due to your generous time, effort, and patience you successfully trained all students to independently travel from home to their College courses. In achieving this all students have gained an invaluable "Life Skill."

Yours sincerely,
Deana Holmes
Barton College, Special Education Coordinator

Written in 2010 by the principal of a mainstream high school that had a special education unit with ten students ranging in age from 14 to 18 years.

Dear Desirée,

We haven't met (hopefully that will be remedied!) but I wanted to write to tell you how grateful I am for what you are doing for Neil. It seems you are having an enormous success with his travel-training, which in turn is having a spill-over effect on his levels of confidence. I'm delighted as it is a most crucial step towards independence.

Over the years of Neil's life, I can count on the fingers of one hand the number of people who have actually done something positive for him. Lots of assessments and fine words but very little action! I am full of admiration that someone like yourself should take so much trouble over the "nitty gritty," and it much raises my estimation of human nature.

There is such a poverty of services for people like Neil and yet with relatively little help they can become more or less independent—a good investment, but it takes patience and vision.

Once again my very sincere thanks,
Beverly Cross

Written in 2000 by a mother whose 14-year-old son was living in a group home.

Dearest Desirée,

We sincerely thank you for your tireless work setting up the school and working with the new teachers and students at the Institute. Independence is not prized, as you know, in this country especially for the disabled, but you somehow managed to help us overcome these cultural barriers and now the children are traveling in their communities confidently and independently with support from their parents and community leaders. The Minister for Education has recently granted us Rs. 10 million to continue the great work of the school for which we are very grateful. Thank you Desirée—we will always remember you as a founder and friend of this school. We look forward to many years' collaboration with you.

Yours sincerely,
Sadia Jedie
Director

Written in 1997 by the director of a school for children
with disabilities in a developing country.

Dear Desirée,

Sincerely—thank you for your support in training our daughter Justine to travel to her special school in Mortdale. You are the kindest most caring person and Justine has really taken a shine to you. You have been a special person in her life. I have now travel-trained Justine to her work experience job at Lakes side, and thank you for your many helpful suggestions. We thank you sincerely for your help and now Justine's confidence in her abilities is growing and travel-training is no longer an insurmountable obstacle. She now travels all the way from home at Beacon to Landsdale (two buses!). Thank you for your wonderful service.

Yours sincerely,
Liz Bensley

Written in 1995 by the mother of a 17-year-old girl.

Dear Desirée,

Just wanted to say thank you with immeasurable gratitude for being an amazing teacher/mentor of travel-training, and the contribution you have made to our school. I cannot begin to thank you enough for the opportunity you gave our teachers, students, and their parents sharing your knowledge and expertise—guiding us to success. I was a little doubtful before I met you about our students learning travel-training skills but thank you for believing in us all and our abilities to succeed.

We hope to see you soon when we commence a new school year with more new students!

Dev Poole
Principal

Written in 1990 by the principal of a special school. The school had approximately 60 children with disabilities, ranging in age from 12 to 19 years.

Limbo

By Cate Kennedy

Why shouldn't a miracle be at the primary school disco
lurching up the dancing queue of the limbo line
where the father of Jayden, the boy with cerebral palsy,
has his arms hooked under his son's, so the boy's almost
walking, almost
dancing
when every boy and every girl, all around the limbo world
is getting ready to shimmy under that broomstick?
The DJ is a seventeen-year-old kid in a
     rainbow vest his mum made him.
He's holding the stick.

I'm watching, for nothing other than the hope
that he doesn't raise it when Jayden's turn arrives
that he keeps it steady as the music says *Hey,*
how low can you go? and one by one the kids tilt
their supple spines backwards, hair dangling,
the jerk and eye-roll, the shudder of splayed muscle
as Chubby Checker croons *liiiimmmmmbbbbooooo*

till it's Jayden's turn; his dad drops to one heavy knee,
slips a hand behind his son's head
and shimmies him under and through—contorted, crooked—
then back up somehow
while the DJ holds that stick immovable, no sleight of hand
and the man does not duck his own head or scramble under
so I can only think—focussed on tipping his boy carefully
into the world beyond, unscathed—
that this father, flexed hard in awkward genuflection
passed through that solid wooden hurdle,
that it dissolved for a single second as his barrel chest breasted it
because, still cupping the frail tendons of his son's neck,
he was suddenly on the other side.

In J. Albiston and K. Brophy (eds.) Prayers of a Secular World.

Victoria, Australia: Inkerman & Blunt Publishers Pty Ltd.

Index

Dr. Desirée Gallimore is the Psychologist/Director of Travel-Training Solutions, and a consultant for parents and professionals on the way to teach safe travel-training for children with intellectual disabilities. She is the Psychologist/Academic Manager for Guide Dogs NSW/ACT, and coordinates the Master of Disability Studies (Sensory Disability) at Macquarie University, Australia. She is also the lead editor of the International Journal of Orientation & Mobility.